The Art
of the
Label

Confectionery label designed by
Lucian Zabel, c. 1928.

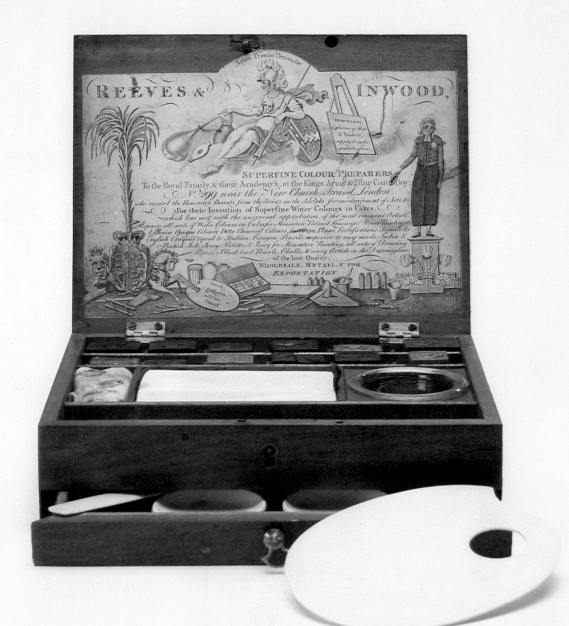

Reeves paintbox, c. 1785.

The Art

of the

Label

Designs of the Times

ROBERT OPIE

CHARTWELL
BOOKS, INC.

A QUARTO BOOK

Published by Chartwell Books Inc
A Division of Book Sales Inc
110 Enterprise Avenue
Secaucus, New Jersey 07094

Copyright © 1987 Quarto Publishing plc

ISBN 1-55521-118-6

This book was designed and produced by
Quarto Publishing plc
The Old Brewery, 6 Blundell Street
London N7 9BH

SENIOR EDITOR Polly Powell
ART EDITOR Vincent Murphy

EDITORS Lisa Hardy, Sandy Shepherd, Henrietta Wilkinson
DESIGNERS Bob Cocker, James Culver
DESIGN ASSISTANT Jacky Morley
PHOTOGRAPHERS Paul Forrester, David Evans
PASTE UP Lawrence Schofield
ART DIRECTOR Moira Clinch
EDITORIAL DIRECTOR Carolyn King

Typeset by Ampersand Ltd, Bournemouth
Manufactured in Hong Kong by Regent Publishing Services Ltd
Printed by Leefung-Asco Printers Ltd, Hong Kong

Quarto Publishing plc would like to take this opportunity to thank the many manufacturers and distributors whose labels appear in this book. It is their patronage and commitment to good design that has made this book possible.

I would like to thank those companies that have assisted my research over many years of collecting, and those friends who have saved examples of consumer products and advertisements for me, especially my mother who has contributed since the quest began in 1963.

ROBERT OPIE

INTRODUCTION

T he paper label must be one of the most abundant of art forms and, taking into account the number of people it reaches, one of the most influential. Most labels are printed for use in their country of origin only, but when a product is exported its printed label can travel to the four corners of the world. By road, rail, sea, and even by camel, the art of the label has been taken far afield on tins of cookies, mustard and canned fruits. For many people, this would have been their first sight of color printing. Many labeled products were distributed in foreign parts by the European powers of the nineteenth century. At first, the colorful and exotic imported brands must have caused much interest abroad, since they reflected a very different way of life. But over time the products became part of the daily scene, so much so that when the makers of Camp coffee decided to alter the label design there was an immediate outcry in India.

Since label design plays such an important role in a product's continuity, it is surprising that manufacturers today allow labels to be vandalized by a clutter of competition announcements and price re-

ductions. One can only suppose that the public are not offended by these recent design changes which are now commonplace in the supermarket – "the gallery of commercial art" – where some 2,000 designs are displayed. The variety is certainly incredible. There are those designs which follow the latest fashion, those which are modern but not "over the top," those which retain much of the tradition of previous generations yet are still stylish, and those which try to look nostalgic. Design apart, the label itself has remained unchanged in its primary function, and the container to which it is attached – matchbox, spirit bottle, or tin can – has altered little since the 1850s, which is remarkable when so many extraordinary changes have happened elsewhere in daily life.

During the history of the label, countless millions of designs have been produced. On matchboxes alone, for example, some 45,000 different label designs have been issued since the time when matchbox production started in Sweden in the 1830s. In England the Christmas cracker firm Batger's produced a range of 88 different box lid labels in a single year (1937). Considering the vast range of goods that used labels,

EGYPT – ACROSS THE DESERT.

and the many manufacturers there have been in all parts of the world, it is almost impossible to estimate the enormous number of designs that must have been created. Among collections of labels worldwide, and taking just two categories, the largest collection of beer labels is over 125,000, and of matchbox labels – over 280,000.

With such a quantity and diversity of labels the task of making a selection for this book has been hard. The main criteria were variety of design, color and ingenuity among the familiar and not-so-familiar consumer products. The labels here are those which best demonstrate the art of the label. The plainer labels and the poorly designed ones are therefore hardly represented. Most of the labels selected come from the period when label designs were being established, between 1880 and 1930, and the main emphasis is on British labels, many of which were exported throughout the world. Even so, American and Continental labels are well represented. In most

Above Trade card, c. 1890 **Left** Basic labeling, c. 1890 **Opposite** "White" labels, c. 1925.

categories it is also possible to see the actual container to which the label was attached.

The labels reproduced here are those which have been attached to a bottle, tin, box, jar, crate or can, rather than being wrappers – which are containers in themselves. Labels that have been excluded are those that do not display the product's name, such as presentation boxes of chocolates where the manufacturer's name is discreetly hidden under the lid.

It has not been possible to cover all product fields, or labels from a wide range of countries so the selection has centered on those areas where the designs are exceptional, including such areas as fruit crate labels and canned foods from America, toiletry labels and twine box labels from France, cookie and confectionery labels from Britain. Some have an international appeal, such as cigar box labels, matchbox labels, and luggage labels.

For social historians, the label is the evidence that certain products existed, and it tells them who the product appealed to and the image it created. Labels also tell them something about a particular era – during the Second World War for instance, the paper shortage caused manufacturers to use smaller labels, and the hoarding instincts of nations in the post-war years were so heightened that for years afterward economy labels were sold by stationers to enable used envelopes to be used once again.

For devotees of label design, and social historians, two books are worthy of note: *Package and Print*, the pioneering work by Alec Davis and *Printed Ephemera* by John Lewis. For those who wish to grasp the intricacies of printing, Michael Twyman's book *Printing 1770–1970* will be invaluable.

Throughout the history of commercial art, little attention or praise has been given to the many illustrators and designers of labels who have created the wonders in this book. In a few cases, distinguished artists have signed their works – Alphonse Mucha, McKnight-Kauffer and, since 1945, the wine labels for each vintage of Château Mouton-Rothschild have been drawn by an eminent artist, including Henry Moore and Salvador Dali. It has been on only rare occasions that the public gaze has turned to this most exuberant form of art. One such occasion was when Andy Warhol turned commercial art into pop art in 1962, and suddenly everyone found themselves looking at a painting of a can of Campbell's soup. For generations commercial art has been looked down on, and little attention has been given to the vital role that packaging plays in modern society (something the Museum of Advertising and Packaging in Gloucester is trying to put right).

Manufacturers have become in-creasingly aware of how important a part the label plays in the sales of their products. Considerable attention is now given to the visual impact of the label, particularly its overall color, this being the first point of visual contact. In the early days, brands were sometimes asked for by their color only, to such an extent that the company would incorporate the color into the brand name. Thus there was Green Label chutney, Carling's Black Label beer, Lyon's Red Label tea and Dewar's White Label whisky.

Manufacturers might remember that the label can become so opulent in comparison with the container's contents, that the customer's expectations are dashed when the contents are revealed. In 1888 when the cigar market in America was moving toward ever more lavish labels, an article on cigars in the *New York Sun* commented ''The label is often better than the cigar …''

ORIGINS AND DEVELOPMENT

I t is easy to speculate on when the earliest paper labels may have been used – a piece of papyrus stuck on an earthenware pot 3,000 years ago, or perhaps a hand-written label on handmade paper made by the Chinese 2,000 years ago. This is quite likely, in a small number of cases. But once paper manufacture had become cheap enough, in the fifteenth century, the humble label would have been stuck on hundreds of bales or containers. It is thought that a leading merchant, Johann Fugger, may have labeled his wares at about this time.

The earliest known printed labels were used during the sixteenth century for bales of cloth. (Labels may have been used on drug phials at this time, but they would probably have been handwritten.) By 1700 printed medicine labels were in use, and possibly wine labels in Italy. There exists a Portuguese port label of 1756, and a German wine label of 1775. Paper-makers were possibly the first to use wrappers with a printed design in the center; it may be that these designs were cut out and used as labels. The German paper-maker Bernhart was using wrappers around 1550.

Until the end of the eighteenth century labels were printed by hand on wooden presses, using handmade paper. In 1798 two inventions led to the proliferation of labels: the paper-

Above left Medicinal label, c. 1790 **Left** Italian cloth merchant's bale label, dated 1695 **Below left** Oil label, typical of 1850-1890 **Above** Stoneware jars and bottles, 1840-1860, with impressed or embossed inscriptions **Far right** Single-color labels dating from 1780-1830.

making machine, invented in France by Nicolas-Louis Robert; and the principle of lithography, discovered by Alois Senefelder in Bavaria. By the 1830s labels were used on all forms of packaging material and on a wide range of products. The next revolution was to be color printing.

The use of color obviously enhanced a label greatly, but it was expensive to have labels colored by hand. For many years inventors tinkered with various methods to find an effective but inexpensive way to print in color. The first satisfactory solution was found by George Baxter, who in 1835 patented his method of color printing from wood engravings onto a monochrome base. By the 1850s the process of chromolithography (the printing on stones of up to twelve different colors by a system of dots and solid areas) had more or less been mastered. This method predominated for the next sixty years, especially in the mass market. Thereafter, developments in printing concentrated on the speed of output and keeping costs down while maintaining quality.

But what were the functions of the label? In the first instance, there was the simple need to say what was inside the pack. The shape of the bottle or jar might already suggest this, but the word "Strawberry," for example, impressed on the side of a jar would identify the type of jam inside it, or the word "Burgess" the name of the manufacturer. Probably the most necessary labeling was for medicines, where it was vital that the contents and directions for use should be seen plainly.

The second aim was to glamorize the pack. A design or pictorial image, particularly if hand-colored, would instantly enliven the overall effect. Some designs were relevant, depicting a scene in which the product was used; some were purely to gain attention using devices such as a beautiful girl. With the arrival of color printing in the 1840s, decorative labels could be mass-produced in a

variety of sizes. They could be stuck onto, say, a box for gloves, which instantly transformed it into a desirable Easter or Christmas present. The appeal of such fancy packs must have encouraged manufacturers to incorporate more decorative designs in their own packaging.

Manufacturers soon noticed that their products sold better if they had an element of prestige attached to them. The presence of the royal coat of arms, a string of medals won at trade exhibitions, or a testimonial from a respected analyst as to a product's purity, gave customers confidence in the quality of what they were buying. By the 1950s a

further sales device was in general use – the direct incentive. Incentives had indeed been in existence since the 1880s when, on Sunlight soap boxes, a £1,000 reward was offered to anyone who could find any impurity in the product. Other inducements were offered at that time, including the pack that had a use after the contents had been consumed, and the label that could be saved and stuck into a scrapbook. But by the end of the 1950s the promotional pack bearing details of a competition, free gift, or price reduction, was commonplace.

Today's supermarket label combines all these ingredients, from the

purely functional message to the inducement, but it must also conform to a string of legal requirements such as the product's ingredients, the sell-by date, and an illustration which is in no way misleading. A further addition is the bar code, necessary for checkout automation, but often tricky for designers to accommodate in the label.

As regards the label itself, there have been few innovations; the exception being in 1935 when Stanton Avery of Los Angeles first manufactured the self-adhesive label. More recently a number of synthetic materials based on plastic properties have been developed to improve the label's wearing quality. The material Polyart, for instance, can resist oil, water and grease, and yet still be printed on by conventional techniques. In many areas the traditional label images are now printed directly onto the can, box or bottle, and this may eventually lead to the disappearance of the familiar paper label.

Top right Soda water bottle, c.1870 **Above right** Crème d'Oranges label (woodcut), c.1810, Honey water label, c.1840, Fry's cocoa label, c.1830 **Right** Matchboxes, 1840-1870.

HAND COLORING

The coloring of labels by hand probably doubled production costs, but for luxury items the price was worth it. Often hand coloring was done by women or children on a production line, with each person adding the next color.

Various hand-colored labels from the first half of the 19th century: **Right** Two French perfume labels from c. 1810, referring to the Napoleonic wars **Far right** Perfume labels, c. 1820 **Below right** Hand-colored box lid for a perfume set, c. 1860 **Below** Crème d'Egypte and Macassar pomade labels, c. 1830 and c. 1840.

ENHANCEMENT

High-quality color printing was available after the 1850s, when chromolithography had reached an acceptable standard. Purely pictorial labels could transform a box of handkerchiefs or perfume into a Christmas gift — and the result would sell as much on the basis of its outward appearance as on the contents. The first to adopt this tactic were the chocolate manufacturers, Fry and Cadbury, in 1868. They used high-quality pictorial labels to help sell their chocolate, particularly at Christmas and Easter.

A decorative label stuck to a box added sales appeal. **Above** Empty boxes whose labels have decorative borders — customers wrote in the contents of the box themselves **Right** A printer's stock book, c. 1860, of finely colored and embossed labels; the central picture was added later. The three boxes with decorative labels are for handkerchiefs, c. 1870, cotton thread, c. 1880, and toilet soap, c. 1890.

In the first half of the 19th century, labels were printed in a single color, usually black, but in the second half color printing became progressively less expensive, and thus more widespread. **Right** A label for Dr. Gregory's powder, c.1860, printed in one color **Far right** Labels for bear's marrow and lime-juice glycerine, c.1860, printed in two colors with gold **Below right** Labels for White Rose, hair oil, rosewater and marrow pomade, c.1865, all using multi-color printing **Below and bottom right** Labels for cognacs, c.1880, using full-color printing.

CONVERSATION PIECES

In France during the nineteenth century there appears to have been a custom for printers in Paris to create frivolous liqueur labels. Sometimes these labels were "branded" by making the liqueur relate to a topical event but, more often, they were inspired on the whim of their creators. These labels were almost certainly intended as conversation pieces. Hundreds of different designs were thought up by the jobbing printer who then touted his labels around the thousands of liqueur distillers (a cottage industry in France even until the 1920s).

Above and **right** Two labels depicting Empress Eugenie (wife of Napoleon III).

Above Bale labels, 1810-1865. In 1862 the American Civil War caused a cotton famine, depicted above.

DIMENSIONS OF THE LABEL

Labels have always had to be versatile. They have been stuck to glass, tin, wood, fabric, plastic, pottery, cardboard and raffia. Moreover, they have been pasted to ribbed surfaces, for example, the Scrubb's ammonia bottle (see page 117).

The largest of the commonly used labels were those inside the lids of wooden display crates, for example some Colman's starch labels of 1900 which measure 15 X 17½in. Labels on the ends of beer barrels were also large, for example the Rhondda Valley Breweries label of c.1920 is 16½in in diameter. The smallest labels were those for medicinal pill boxes such as that for the one-penny tin of Howell's chocolate pills, which is ⅘in in diameter.

When the Intoxicating Liquors (Sale to Children) Act came into force in England in 1901, it became necessary for all bottles which could be easily opened to have paper seals over their tops. This device made them tamper-evident and was applied particularly to the screw stoppers (introduced in 1885) used by the beer trade.

Most labels conform to the traditional and economical square or oblong shape, but there have been variations, such as the Holbrook's Punch sauce label (see page 89) and Robertson's lemon-shaped Silver Shred label. Oval labels were pre-

ferred for drinks bottles such as beers, but in the 1960s the speeding up of the bottle labeling process meant that labels required straight edges to enable the machines to pick them up. In order to retain the oval look, and yet conform to the rectangular format now required, black borders were added – the blackness blending in with the dark bottle (examples of this design include the Guinness labels on page 64).

Labels could also be stuck onto a variety of places on a bottle. The bottle for Benedictine liqueur at one time sported five separate labels. Most sauce labels went around three sides of the bottle. For Izal, "the universal germicide" (see page 117), a separate label was pasted to each of the bottle's sloping sides, none of which obviously acted as the main label. The strangest place to put a label is probably on the base of the bottle, but even this was done, with Dear Brothers malt vinegar. A round label was added to the underside of the octagonal bottle, which informed those pouring the vinegar that it "conformed with the requirements of the Foods and Drugs Acts and all regulations relating thereto."

Top Medicine tax label, c.1920; stopper seal, c.1915 **Left** Labels for VO5 shampoo, 1986, printed on both sides so that the main image is viewed through the liquid shampoo (similar to the technique previously used on the novelty perfume ashtray, c.1955) **Below** Silver Shred label, c.1905.

STOCK LABELS

During the nineteenth century most commodities were delivered in bulk to the retailer or local wholesaler. Dried fruit, rice, tea, coffee and many other commodities would be weighed out and wrapped to each customer's needs. In the case of liquid products such as wine, whisky, port, cordials, vinegar, jams or honey, the items were pre-bottled or jarred by the retailer in large enough quantities to stock his

shelves. Each bottle and jar would then be labeled according to its contents. These labels were often purchased from a local printer who had ready supplies of the required type, and for an extra charge the printer would add the retailer's name and address to the stock label. Much the same practice applied to the druggist, with his many potions, pills and poisons.

From such small beginnings many retailers expanded to become manufacturers in their own right (the classic example being Jesse Boot, the druggist who founded the Boots chain). They therefore required their own unique labels for their individual brands.

Generally speaking, labels without a manufacturer's name on them or an over-printed retailer's name, were likely to be printers' stock labels, even though a brand name may have appeared in the design (for example, "Seasons" Brand salmon and the "Poppy" Brand pineapple

chunks, shown opposite). Some brand names were also used in a generic sense for products such as "Garibaldi" cookies or "Easton's Syrup", a lethal-sounding concoction of "phosphate of iron with quinine and strychnine."

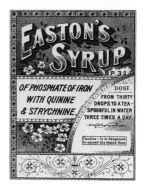

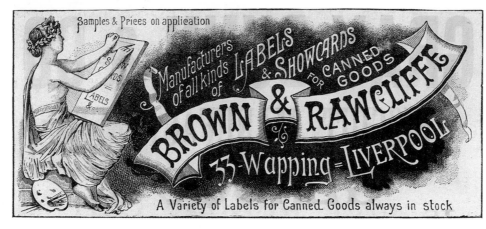

Above left Stock label for chemist, c. 1870 **Left** Printer's advertisement, 1885 **Top** Stock label for cordial, c. 1905 **Above** Label for Easton's syrup designed c. 1900.

Below Printer's leaflet, c. 1910
Right Printer's leaflet, c. 1920,
with labels designed some 20
years earlier.

Above and opposite Printers' stock labels, c. 1930: two pages from the catalog of J. & J. Murdock Ltd of Glasgow.

LABELS FOR PROMOTION

Drinks labels, particularly those for beer, have often been enlarged and used as advertisements, without any additional slogans or supporting image. Two examples are McEwan's beer and Fremlin's beer. Other beer companies, such as Guinness, Allsopp and Bass, used the single label as an advertisement. Labels have often been included as part of the design of pub promotional accessories. The fancy Dunville's label etched onto a whisky glass, the Allsopp's coaster and the Worthington's ashtray are all examples of these promotional uses.

Above right McEwan's enamel sign, c. 1900 **Above** Fremlin's tin sign, c. 1920 **Right** Pub promotional items: Dunville's glass, c. 1900; Allsopp's jug stand or "coaster," c. 1896; Worthington's ashtray, c. 1930.

MINIATURES

In an attempt to encourage the public to sample their wares, manufacturers produced miniature bottles, jars and cans of their products. These were distributed at exhibitions, given by the retailer to his customers, or sent to those who wrote in response to an advertisement.

Miniature containers from 1910 to 1935, together with a giant Rose's Lime Juice display bottle (c. 1920). The Black & White whisky bottle has its own miniature corkscrew. The Guinness bottle is deceptive — it contained eau-de-Cologne and was produced by Cussons, Sons & Co. Ltd in 1925.

INTERNATIONAL IMAGE

Fortunately for the global traveler, a pictorial message is recognizable in any country: it is possible to pick out products from pictures on the label whether in South America or Japan. Many brands known to the traveler at home are now sold internationally, and can be picked out not only by the familiar design of their label, but also by the presence of the motif (or ''logo'') used by the company. The design and logo may have been absorbed only subconsciously by the shopper, yet they are instantly recognized and instantly convey a feeling of trust and reassurance. The ''keystone'' logo of Heinz products, for example, has been familiar to people around the world for over 80 years. Similarly, the design and vivid yellow of the Colman's mustard label has been an internationally recognized image since the early years of the twentieth century.

Above Small promotional booklet showing a Heinz can with overwrap, c. 1900.

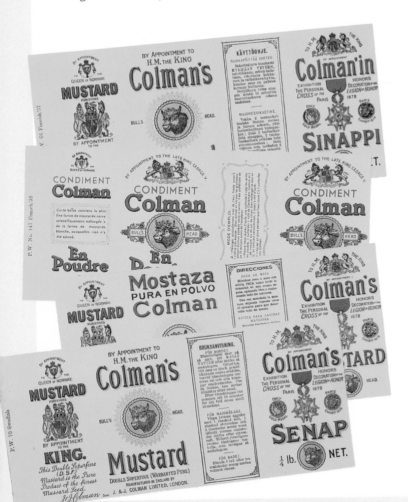

Left Colman's mustard labels, c.1935, for Finland, France, South America and Sweden.

Above Heinz products of the 1930s using the "keystone" logo and the gherkin trademark.

FROM BOTTLES TO STORAGE JARS

U ntil comparatively recently, there has been a stigma attached to the world of trade, and most store-bought products were decanted into a non-commercial container before they reached the dining-room table. One advantage of the label was that it could be soaked off easily, thus removing the offending trade name.

For hundreds of years, however, containers for products have often become as valuable as their contents. Indeed, bottles and crates were frequently re-used and deposits paid on purchase to encourage their return. The use of cracker boxes or Oxo tins for storage has now become part of the domestic scene, and jam jars have made excel-

lent carriers for goldfish or minnows. With this idea in mind, some manufacturers have promoted their packaging as having an after-use. Some toffee tins, for instance, have been designed to be converted into receptacles for flour, sugar, tea or rice, these names being printed on the reverse side of the tin. Similarly, Ronuk's furniture cream pot became a desirable blue vase and Schweppe's lemon squash bottle a fine whisky decanter.

During the late 1960s this form of promotion became particularly active, when jam and coffee jars turned neatly into drinking tumblers or storage containers, a practice that the instant coffee manufacturers continue to this day.

Above left and **left** Glass decanters and pottery jars, c. 1930 **Below** Mugs from the 1960s.

DESIGNED FOR COLLECTING

Another form of promotion requiring the removal of labels was aimed at people's instinct for collecting. From the mid-1880s, and for about 30 years thereafter, Colman's issued series of attractive pictorial labels on the lids of their starch boxes, aimed primarily at children. Some of these labels were simply pretty pictures, but Colman's probably felt morally bound to issue most of their series with an educational slant, especially since the promotional message of "Colman's Starch" ended up in the scrapbook as well. In this way, labels were issued, sometimes as frequently as one a week, on subjects ranging from the identification of butterflies to (in a series of 30 labels) the life of Edward VII on his accession to the throne in 1901. Other starch manufacturers, such as Reckitt and Hydroleine, took up the idea of pictorial lids, as can be seen below.

Above right Labels for oval 1oz tins of Colman's mustard, introduced in 1886. By 1900 a series of 22 national flags had been established.

Right and **below** Starch boxes with pictorial lids, c.1900. Children were encouraged to soak these off to put in their scrapbooks. The box for Stiff's starch was one of 10 in a wedding series; this one is entitled "Realization" **Bottom right** Dent's collar boxes, c.1900

WARTIME RESTRICTIONS

There were numerous restrictions on the use of raw materials during the Second World War, which had major effects on packaging. By the early 1940s labels on all forms of container had been reduced in size to save paper. Label designs were adapted to the slimmer format, and less color (or strength of color) was used to save on printer's ink. Sometimes the labels for the smaller sizes of bottles or jars could also be used on larger sizes.

In the case of Bluebell metal polish, a small paper label was attached to the tin instead of being printed all over it; with the small sizes of Bluebell and Brasso, the normal tin was changed to a glass bottle with a label.

Paper restrictions during the Second World War meant that many of these overwraps were permanently discontinued, although today the vulnerable toothpaste tube is still packaged in a box, as are some shampoo and medicine bottles.

Developments in packaging now mean that· there are fewer spoiled

labels (the exceptions being sold off at a reduced price by the supermarkets). For instance, the problem of scuffed jam jar labels was recently solved when the jar was slightly waisted where the label is attached — no longer need the labels rub against each other during transit.

ALL WRAPPED UP

During the last hundred years many bottled products have been sold with their own individual outer box or wrapper. Originally this addition was intended to provide extra protection for the glass container, but it also meant that the label of the product within was fresh and clean when unwrapped at its final destination in the customer's home. In the mind of the customer, the product would seem untouched by other hands, and carefully preserved for them alone. Perhaps, too, the actual sensation of opening a box or unwrapping a bottle conjured up pleasant associations with the unwrapping of presents on birthdays and at Christmas.

Outer wrappers either had an exact replica of the inner label printed on them, or the inner label would be stuck onto a plain outer wrapper, as with Robertson's Golden Shred marmalade (see page 93).

Top Products from the early 1940s with "reduced" labels
Left Products with overwraps, from the 1920s. The traditional medicinal label was black printed on white, but an outer box or wrapper could carry a more colorful presentation without disturbing the familiar label on the product. (Other examples of overwraps include the Horlicks and Ovaltine tins illustrated on page 70 and the Heinz tomato soup can on page 22.)

THE DECLINE OF THE PAPER LABEL

The versatility of the paper label, its ability to be stuck to almost any surface and the ease and cheapness of its production, has made it a popular and widespread packaging tool. Yet even as its use spread, there were areas in which it was already being replaced by other forms of packaging.

Labels for ceramic pot lids were in use through most of the nineteenth century, but by the middle of the century advances made in the transfer printing of pot lids meant that there was a steady decline in the use of paper labels. By the 1880s they were no longer used for the lids of most tooth powders, cold creams and bear's grease (hair cream). Even though transfer printing with an overglaze was more expensive, the advantage of not using an easily-soiled label was thought to be worthwhile.

By 1910 there were a number of matchbox labels being printed direct-ly onto the card sides, although this transition was slow and England's Glory, for instance, remained with a pasted-on label until the 1950s.

Many other products were also taking advantage of direct printing and by the 1960s most cheese boxes had lost their lid labels, although the individual triangles of cheese inside still bear their labels to this day.

Within the perfume and toiletry markets, labels diminished in size and flamboyancy, relying more for their glamour on the shape and appearance of the jar or bottle. Today much use is made of direct printing on glass for perfume bottles, and the self-adhesive label for toiletries.

The possibilities of art on the label were greatly reduced by the demise of the large labels pasted on cookie tins (see pages 78-83), fruit crates (see pages 102-105) and those used as advertisements on the inside of the lids of wooden display boxes (see pages 74-75). The American fruit crate label was also a victim of the wartime rationing of the 1940s and

was replaced with a two-color stamp on the end of the crate. The wooden display boxes with labels pasted inside their hinged lids were in use through to the 1930s. The display box used to be seen on the grocer's counter with the lid open to reveal its advertising label and its contents of, say, two dozen cans of metal polish, or Fry's chocolate drops for sale loose by the quarter pound. When these boxes went out of fashion the art of their labels became extinct.

Left Printing directly onto the pack – only the top packs have paper labels **Above right** Doing without bottle labels: the image on the beer bottle, c. 1939, has been "fired on," and the image on the whisky bottle, c. 1950, has been silk-screen printed.

DESIGN

During the eighteenth century the main strength of commercial design lay with the copper engravers who fashioned their elegant label designs from material that already existed – book plates and invitation cards, shopkeepers' billheads and trade cards. The painter William Hogarth (1697-1764) was one of the many engravers involved in commercial work at this time.

By contrast, the wood engraver's work was primitive. Wood engraving was a cheaper method, and was favored for the production of tobacco wrappers. This has always been the manufacturer's dilemma – keeping down the costs on the throwaway pack without jeopardizing the feeling of quality of the product.

It should be mentioned, however, that tobacco wrappers were also copper-engraved (numerous examples of wood- and copper-engraved wrappers can be seen in John Lewis's book *Printed Ephemera*). By 1800 the skill of Thomas Bewick (1753-1828) had enhanced this art greatly, and in America Alexander Anderson (1775-1870) was inspired by

Bewick's work to make his own designs.

As the labeling of containers became more widespread in the nineteenth century printing technology made continuous progress, and the label designers made use of these advances. The early Lucifer matchboxes, for instance, were produced in the style of the security printing used for lottery tickets and bank notes, a technique made possible by the newly developed compound plate printer.

It was probably during the 1830s and 1840s that printers in England

Left In the 1820s Robert Branston designed many labels for Japan blacking, stylized after the lottery ticket. A feature of this label is the oversized street-number of the manufacturer **Below left** Martell cognac label, 1877 **Below** Woodcut design for toothpowder, probably by Bewick, c. 1790 **Bottom** Sarti design by Cappiello, c. 1930.

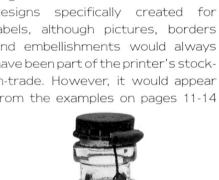

began to establish their stocks of designs specifically created for labels, although pictures, borders and embellishments would always have been part of the printer's stock-in-trade. However, it would appear from the examples on pages 11-14 that French printers in Paris had established a trade in pictorial liqueur and perfume labels at an earlier date.

The Great Exhibition held in Hyde Park, London, during the summer of 1851, prompted many manufacturers to create something special for their displays which were going to be seen by representatives from all over the world. Huntley & Palmer's, for example, commissioned White & Pike of Birmingham to devise a new label, and as a result the famous Garter and Buckle trade mark was born (see page 80). It was still in use in the 1950s. The noted industrial designer, Owen Jones, was also involved with Huntley & Palmer's labels during the 1860s, and in 1863 he designed a label for Allsopp's ales.

The arrival of cheaper, high-quality printing transformed label design

pasted around a small object, the writing on them could be read only by constantly turning the container. In the cases of Crosse & Blackwell's Mushroom Catsup, and Pond's Extract, the labels were wrapped around the bottle, making the writing vertical. This may have saved the expense of separate front and back labels, but it did mean that it was essential to keep the top on while reading the instructions.

Above left Schlesinger's Turkish emery polishing power, c.1890, and Sanitas shaving stick, c.1900 **Below left** Crosse & Blackwell's catsup, c.1900, and Pond's extract, c.1910 **Below** Carr's furniture polish with additional "offer" label.

over the next thirty years, evidence of which can be seen throughout this book. The full potential of the label as an artistic form was at last being explored, although it is only in recent years that it has become recognized as an art form worthy of study.

As new brands ventured onto the widening and highly competitive markets of the 1870s and 1880s, careful consideration was given to the design of labels, for it was appreciated that an unvarying and dependable image spoke well for the quality of the product to which it was attached. One of the longest-serving labels was that for Martell cognac, designed in 1848 and dropped in favor of a more contemporary style only in 1968.

Yet among all the successful designs there were many oddities. Labels which looked acceptable when flat were less effective when

LABEL ADAPTATION

It is self-evident that a shop-keeper's livelihood depends upon his ability to sell his wares. In the past it rested with his ability to buy, wrap and successfully promote his goods. Gradually, however, with the increase of pre-packaged merchandise, the manufacturer took over much of the responsibility for selling the goods by organizing national sales campaigns in newspapers and on hoardings. By the

1890s the increasing flood of new products was accompanied by a mass of promotional material for the retail outlets — display cards, cardboard novelties and leaflets.

At this time, no sales promotion was allowed to feature on the package itself. The package design was, in a sense, a fixed asset; it was to be built on, carefully up-dated and altered only occasionally — certainly not to be disfigured by vulgar announcements of offers which would destroy the overall image.

During the next 40 years, manufacturers tucked their promotional literature for each product inside outer wrappers or underneath tin

lids. To announce a free canister offer, Carr attached a paper slip to each furniture polish jar. By the 1930s some companies had begun to add "flash" announcements to the front of their packs.

However, it was the coming of the self-service store in the 1950s that meant that the marketing message finally landed fully on the label. The shopkeeper no longer had direct control over the customer's purchase; it was the customer who now chose the product from the ranks of silent salesmen. The appeal of the pack had become paramount, and part of that appeal was the "6¢ Off," "Win $1,000" or "Free Stockings" flash.

Above left Label extensions used to accommodate additional information, 1987 **Left** A new design for Gale's orange curd, 1984, allows the inclusion of a bar code **Above** The old Vimto design (1930s) is incorporated into the new (1950s), to maintain product recognition **Right** Labels with promotional additions for cans of Heinz baked beans 1965-1987.

ART NOUVEAU

One of the first major influences on label design was the Art Nouveau movement, at the height of its popularity between 1895-1915. This style was used mainly for products in the perfume and toiletry markets, but many new packaged brands launched during this period were affected. Such was the case with the Kop's cream puddings label, which typifies the flowing organic lines of the time.

ART DECO

In sharp contrast to the Art Nouveau style, Art Deco mixed vivid colors with angular lines. This new wave of design gathered momentum during the 1920s. As with Art Nouveau, the labels primarily affected were those for toiletries, although the labels for Radio Malt and CWS's Lustre cigarettes were also affected by the movement, both using a sunburst motif.

1950s

During the 1950s there was a trend to get rid of the embellishments and intricacies of the Victorian and Edwardian designers and to make packaging design simpler. This was the continuation of a movement begun in the 1930s, and typified by the label for Lyons coffee (**right**) which has, incidentally, an early use of the "sell by" date (on the individual container rather than the outer crate). After World War II the trend continued, spurred on by the growing number of self-service stores, where customers themselves had to pick out the desired brand among its competitor-products. **Below** One of the leading packaging designers during the 1950s was Milner Gray, three of whose labels are shown here **Opposite page** Different label styles from the 1950s.

TO MAKE Coffee for two persons, put two heaped dessertspoonfuls of Lyons Coffee into a hot earthenware jug. Pour on half a pint of freshly boiling water. Stir vigorously, stand for one minute. Draw the edge of a spoon gently across the surface to settle the grounds floating on the top. Allow to stand for a further four minutes. Pour slowly and steadily into another hot earthenware jug. We recommend serving half Coffee, half hot (not boiled) Milk

J. LYONS & CO. LTD., CADBY HALL, LONDON, W.14

LYONS COFFEE

AS THIS COFFEE IS NOT VACUUM PACKED, IT SHOULD BE SOLD BEFORE OCT. 17, 1942

HALF POUND NET

DOUBLE COURAGE
BREWED & BOTTLED BY COURAGE & CO LTD LONDON
OLD ALE
BREWERS SINCE 1787

GILBEY'S SQUADRON RUM

SHIPPED AND BOTTLED BY
W & A Gilbey
LIMITED LONDON NW1 ENGLAND
70° PROOF Produce of the West Indies

BONNIE CHARLIE SCOTCH WHISKY
BLENDED & BOTTLED BY CHARLES KINLOCH & CO LTD LONDON & EDINBURGH ESTABLISHED 1861
70° PROOF 26⅔ FL OZS

1960s

By the 1960s, label designers resorted to many ways to get the message across: sometimes it was large, bold words; at others, a graphic image or photographic illustration (as on Sainsbury's spaghetti and ground steak) emphasized the container's contents. At this time, promotional incentives took off, from the straightforward "5d off" to the redeemable voucher, for example, the Crosse & Blackwell's soup label of 1961. By the end of the 1960s shampoo and squash bottles were moving to plastic, for example, the Robinson's bottle, with its imitation child's art label.

Baked beans cans, 1979-82. At the end of the 1970s, International Stores introduced their "no frills" product range. The labels for these cheaper products reflected this approach.

1970s

Design among the supermarket chains was more progressive than that of established brands, where caution was required when modifying label design. Thus in the 1970s, "own label" designs extended the use of symbolism to convey the container's contents, often a rather stark image. The label for an up-market product, such as lobster soup, required more detailed treatment. Even so, photographic images were much in evidence.

Dougal from the children's television series "Magic Roundabout" was used around a can of dog food in 1973, the same year that Biba were labeling baked beans with their dramatic gold-on-black design.

1980s

Today, there is a new awareness of the importance packaging plays in the sale of goods, promoted by such designers as Peter Windett (Crabtree & Evelyn, **below**) and Michael Peters. For 20 years or more, established brands had been making minor updates to their sacred images. However, the label in its most modern idiom is primarily still the preserve of the supermarket chains whose "own label" brands embrace the latest design trends. Labels for such mundane products as fabric conditioner, toilet cleaner and dishwashing liquid now appear to be worthy of less mundane design.

Right Two examples of art at its most entertaining, targeted at children: Noodle Doodles, 1986; St. Michael baked beans, 1982.

Below Designs which hark back to the Victorian era. Nostalgic, perhaps, but they do capture the spirit of a time when brands were originally promoted as being pure and wholesome. Sometimes the label has been created from inspiration; at other times it has been lifted straight from the past, as with the lemonade label.

Below A mixture of modern styles, 1987, from the delicate Waitrose honey label to the flamboyant Tesco vodka label.

Health and Beauty

Medicines · Perfumes · Toiletries

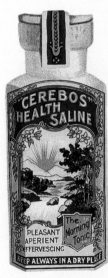

Detail from showcard, c. 1905.

MEDICINES

All the pills, powders and potions ever made have needed containers of some sort: there have been glass phials and bottles, stone pots and jars, paper wrappers and cardboard or wooden boxes. The earliest known medicine labels were those attached to medicinal phials. At first they were hand-inscribed, but by the seventeenth century crudely printed labels appeared on them. By 1800 labels were also being pasted to the lids of chipwood or cardboard boxes.

On the whole, people put their faith in whatever cure claimed to be the most beneficial. In the nineteenth century, vast fortunes were made by men like Parkinson (whose company was promoted as the world's largest pill producer; in 1895 it sold 2,519,856 boxes of sugar-coated pills). Similarly, Thomas Holloway made a fortune by selling pills and ointments and, when he died in 1883, left an endowment of over one million pounds to set up a sanatorium and a college for women. At the same time there were companies such as Burroughs Wellcome, which was set up in London in 1880 by two American pharmacists to produce bona fide medicines. These companies helped to save the reputation of the pharmaceutical industry.

Lozenge box labels, 1820-1830.

MEDICINAL LABELS

The astonishing range of cures was equaled only by the variety of typefaces used in their label design. Medicinal manufacturers would often wrap their products in promotional literature which described the wonders of the cures. Occasionally there would be a testimonial on the label, as with Laverack's Instant Relief for Unbroken Chilblains (**far left**) — where the puff is so full of praise that the manufacturer has had to insert a note of caution. The graphics illustrated on this page are typical of the 1890s, but the styles remained essentially unchanged up until the 1950s.

Left A pleasing label might be thought to help counter the taste of cod-liver oil or a cough-cure syrup: the label for Children's Fever Cure, c. 1925, (**below**) incorporates a photographic image. Mellin's emulsion, c. 1905.

PARKINSON'S

Parkinson's was established in 1848, and became one of the largest medicinal companies in the world. It also made numerous other products, from boot polish to custard powder. The Parkinson's labels featured a vigorous combination of design and color, and in some instances incorporated the portrait of the founder, R. Parkinson. The labels shown here are from the 1880s and 1890s.

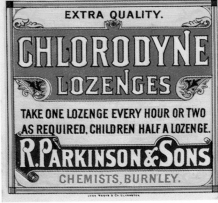

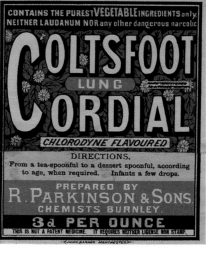

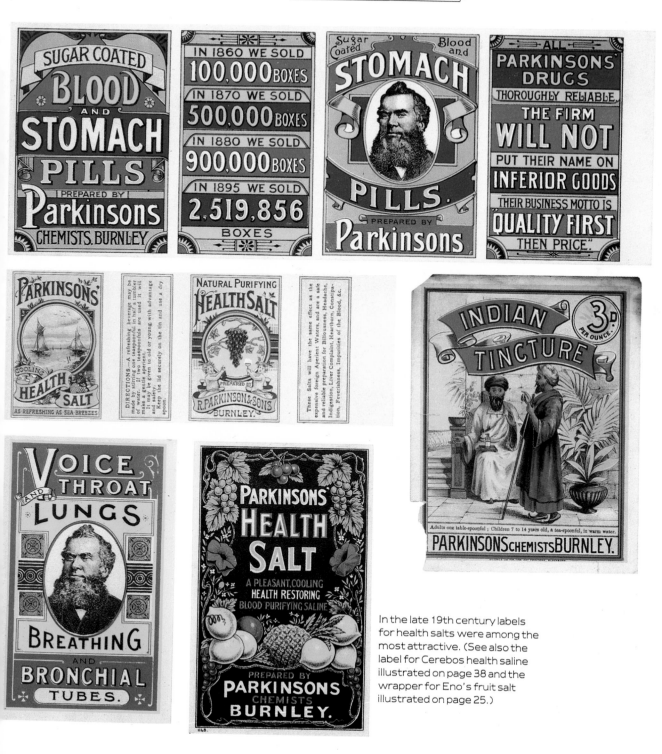

SUGAR COATED BLOOD AND STOMACH PILLS PREPARED BY Parkinsons CHEMISTS, BURNLEY

IN 1860 WE SOLD 100,000 BOXES
IN 1870 WE SOLD 500,000 BOXES
IN 1880 WE SOLD 900,000 BOXES
IN 1895 WE SOLD 2,519,856 BOXES

Sugar Coated Blood and STOMACH PILLS. PREPARED BY Parkinsons

ALL PARKINSONS' DRUGS THOROUGHLY RELIABLE. THE FIRM WILL NOT PUT THEIR NAME ON INFERIOR GOODS THEIR BUSINESS MOTTO IS "QUALITY FIRST THEN PRICE."

PARKINSONS' COOLING HEALTH SALT AS REFRESHING AS SEA BREEZES

NATURAL PURIFYING HEALTH SALT PREPARED BY R. PARKINSON & SONS BURNLEY.

INDIAN TINCTURE 3D PER OUNCE
Adults one table-spoonful ; Children 7 to 14 years old, a tea-spoonful, in warm water.
PARKINSONS CHEMISTS BURNLEY.

VOICE THROAT AND LUNGS BREATHING AND BRONCHIAL TUBES.

PARKINSONS' HEALTH SALT A PLEASANT, COOLING HEALTH RESTORING BLOOD PURIFYING SALINE PREPARED BY PARKINSONS CHEMISTS BURNLEY.

In the late 19th century labels for health salts were among the most attractive. (See also the label for Cerebos health saline illustrated on page 38 and the wrapper for Eno's fruit salt illustrated on page 25.)

PERFUMES

When the Egyptians invented glass bottles around 1000 BC, they were usually used for perfumes. The Greeks made shaped glass perfume bottles, a tradition carried on by the Venetian glassmakers in the thirteenth century.

In the nineteenth century there were many established perfume companies in France and Britain which vied with each other to capture the fashionable scent market, such as Rimmel and Grossmith. Today the shaped bottle still plays an important role in the product's appeal.

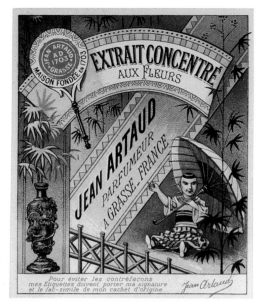

The essence of packaging for the boudoir was – and still is – to make the item look chic and, preferably, expensive. Any product, whether it was a perfume, toilet water, lotion, face cream or powder, needed to sit pretty on the dressing table. These French labels date from 1905-20.

In Edwardian days small bottles of perfume were sold in snug boxes that were in themselves often highly decorative. The bottles' glass stoppers were covered by a cloth top held in place by a ribbon and a neck label. The bottles shown here date from the period 1895-1925. Of particular interest is the bottle for Perfumes of the Empire: S. Africa (**left center**) with its spelling error. The opaque orange-colored bottle for Cologne Russe (**left**) makes an ideal setting for the label.

Art Deco perfume labels from 1925-30. Apart from the scent itself, perfume manufacturers rely on their reputation and the visual impact of the packaging to sell their products. The design can be changed far more frequently and far more radically than in other areas of manufacture.

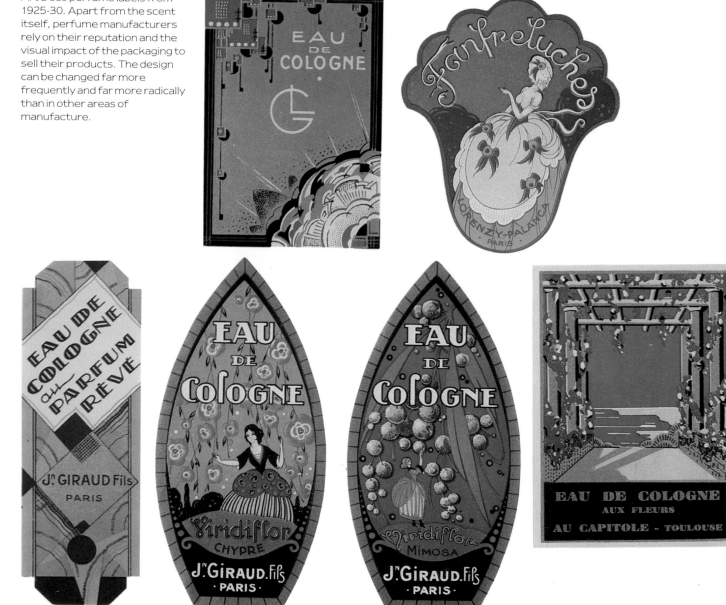

4711 LABELS

The use of blue (in different strengths) with gold has created a continuity of style across the whole range of 4711 products, even though the individual designs are quite varied. The 4711 labels shown here are from the 1930s, but the color combination is still in use today. The number 4711 is alleged to have been the secret formula for making *aqua mirabilis* (miracle water) told to the company's founder, Ferdinand Muhlens, by a monk to whom he had given refuge. **Above left** Lid of a face-powder box **Left** Lid of the 1935 eau-de-Cologne presentation case.

TOILETRIES

Throughout history there has been a constant demand for preparations that enhanced the human face and hid the ravages of time or illness. The vanity of women — and men — has turned them to beautifying, cleansing or masking preparations to improve their appearance.

During the nineteenth century many toiletry companies like Yardley (founded in 1770), Pears (1789) and Atkinson (1799) were establishing their reputations. Unlike many toiletries in the past, their creams and soaps did not contain harmful additives. In America the beauty parlor had become widespread by the end of the century. Max Factor set up his business in Hollywood in 1908 and two years later Elizabeth Arden opened her first salon in New York.

Bouquet and toiletry labels from 1830 (**top**) to 1870 (**bottom**). The label for Royal vegetable essence has been hand-colored. The Court bouquet label uses a similar design surround as the garter and buckle design of Huntley & Palmer's label on page 80.

These labels were designed for boxes of toilet soaps produced by Blondeau & Co. (later known as Vinolia), and were printed in no fewer than 12 colors. They were reproduced in the 1898 specimen catalog of Alf Cooke of Leeds, a leading printing company which billed itself as the "largest, cleanest, healthiest and most completely fitted printing works in the world... with 300 chromo-litho and other machines." On their advanced machinery it was possible to print up to 17 colors.

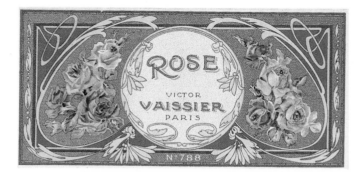

Labels for boxes of French toilet soap, dating from 1900–1920. The artists drew heavily on the Art Nouveau style, creating countless flamboyant designs. Each box contained three individually wrapped bars of soap.

Putting a single brand-name on a complete range of toiletries is popular, the theory being that it encourages the customer to stick to a single manufacturer's products. Thus Boots used the name "Regesan" and Atkinson used "Californian Poppy." Elizabeth Arden built up its range of "Venetian" products between 1915 and 1920, the labels being "pure and simple," a trend continued by Chanel in 1921.

Left Cold creams, c. 1925 **Below** Elizabeth Arden's Venetian range, c. 1925.

HAIR TONICS AND BRILLIANTINES

By the 1850s tonics for promoting the growth of hair were popular, and in the 1880s brilliantine, to give the hair extra gloss, arrived.

By the end of the 1920s manufacturers were using small labels for perfumes and toiletries, such as those for the brilliantines of Coty and Jules Frères (**below**).

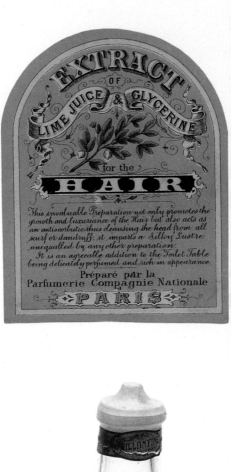

TOOTHPASTE

During Victorian times it was customary to clean one's teeth with soot or salt, but toothpowder, utilizing the cleansing properties of areca nut, came increasingly into vogue. At first the ceramic toothpowder pots had paper labels, but after 1870 labels like these were generally replaced by designs printed in black directly onto the lid. **Below** Paper band designed to seal the pot-lid to its base.

DRINKS

EARLY SPIRITS · WHISKY · GIN · COCKTAILS

WINE BRANDY AND RUM · BEER · SPA WATER

SOFT DRINKS AND SQUASHES · COFFEE

TEA AND HEALTH DRINKS · COCOA

Shelvey's fruit syrup, c. 1900.

EARLY SPIRITS

It is possible that the Chinese were distilling spirits from rice around 1000 BC, but the distillation of spirits from corn was invented in Europe around AD 1100. Even then it was not for another 400 years that an acceptable result was really achieved. The art of distilling was practiced by the monks and the apothecaries, who added the spirits to their potions. When the monasteries in England were dissolved by Henry VIII in 1539, much of this knowledge was dispersed, and slowly commercial distillers became established.

It was not until the 1850s that whisky and gin started to be individually bottled and it became necessary to label each bottle. The labels were either the manufacturer's own or purchased from a local printer's stock.

Printers' stock labels from c.1870. The label for strong mixing gin has a space ready for the distiller's or distributor's name to be inserted. Old Tom was an artificially sweetened gin; its label was printed by J. Cross & Son of London, who registered the design at Stationers' Hall to prevent others from using it. (This protected it under the Fine Arts Copyright Act of 1862; such registration became unnecessary after the Imperial Copyright Act of 1911.)

WHISKY

The commercial production of whisky began around 1500, but it remained a cottage industry for over 300 years. During the second half of the nineteenth century Scotch whisky rapidly grew in popularity, first in Britain and then as a world-wide export. John Haig built a distillery in 1824, John Dewar set up his Perth-based business in 1846 and William Teacher started up in Glasgow in 1830. In Ireland the major distillers were established earlier; John Jameson in 1780 and John Power in 1791.

Whisky bottles dating from 1900-1940.

GIN

Up until the sixteenth century gin was mainly produced by the monasteries, or by alchemists, and was used as a medicine. It was also given to soldiers before battle — hence the expression "Dutch courage." Commercial production of gin started in 1575 when Lucas Bols founded his distillery in Schiedam.

Dutch gin bottles of c. 1900. The bottles were uniformly square to make transportation easier.

English gin bottles dating from 1910 to 1950. Distinctive bottle-shapes and labels were used to help barmen identify the products quickly.

COCKTAILS

Originating in America during the early years of the nineteenth century, the cocktail is a combination of three or more ingredients shaken or stirred together. The main contenders for this concoction are gin, vermouth, sherry, brandy or whisky along with bitters, crème, fruit juice or an egg white.

The first book on cocktails, *The Bon Vivant's Guide or How to Mix Drinks*, was published in America in 1862, but the craze for them did not take off until the 1920s. Ironically, it was probably the prohibition of liquor in the US (which came into force in 1919) that popularized cocktails — they disguised the presence of the forbidden alcohol. By the 1930s ready-mixed branded cocktails were widely available, such as Bronx and Manhattan, and their bottles were often exotically shaped.

The cocktail bottles of the 1920s and 1930s came in exotic shapes. Gordon's "ready to serve" cocktails were dispensed from a mixer shaped bottle, and their miniature sizes were a scaled-down version complete with three mini labels.

WINE

The ancient Egyptians enjoyed wine, as did the Greeks almost 3,000 years ago. The Greeks stored their wines in open earthenware vessels (amphorae); the Romans improved on this by developing barrels and bottles for storage. By AD400 vineyards had been established in France and Germany. During the seventeenth century the quality of wine was greatly improved when cork stoppers were used. Soon after, the glass industry was re-established and glass bottles were produced. Wine bottles at this time had long necks and wide, rounded bases (much the same shape as an onion); by 1800 the wine bottle had developed into the familiar shape of those in the stores today, and labels began to be used. Some Italian wines may have been labeled from as early as 1700 and German wines from the 1770s. Champagne and Bordeaux began to be labeled in the 1830s.

Designs for wine labels have in the past been traditional in style. The wine connoisseur was supposed to find inspiration in the bouquet and taste, not the label. There were exceptions, like the label of c. 1935 (**left**). Today, wine labels show a wider range of styles as can be seen on the bottle of Beaujolais Nouveau, 1986 (**below**). Occasionally a wine label indicates the geographical location of the vineyard, for example the Beaujolais label of c. 1880, (**below left**). Most wines carry the year of vintage, often on a neck label. The champagne labels (**below left**) date from around 1910.

BRANDY AND RUM

Brandy is known to have been distilled, most commonly in Italian monasteries more than a thousand years ago. Its use then was as it often still is, medicinal.

In the testimonial for a "Pale Eau de Vie" brandy produced by Henry Brett in 1867, part of the analyst's report states that it "is fit for all purposes — Dietetical and Medical — for which the Brandies of France have hitherto been used."

During the eighteenth century, a distillation of sugar cane began to arrive in Europe — rum. It was imported from the West Indies where, since the mid-seventeenth century, it had been given to the laborers in the sugar cane plantations to keep

Two examples of die-cut labels: **Above** Fine Old Brown brandy, c. 1870 **Right** A. J. Bellot cognac label produced to commemorate the centenary (1876) of American Independence Day.

Above Two "Rhum Vieux" labels, examples of French stock designs (c. 1910).

them content. Since then, Jamaica has been the main supplier of rum to Britain, whose sailors in the Navy received a daily tot of rum until 1970. The French have always been fond of *rhum*, receiving it mainly from Martinique and Guadeloupe.

Puerto Rico was the main source of sugar cane for the making of rum in the United States, where it was the first major liquor to be distilled (from about 1700). Barbados is noted for its light rum.

French and Italian (Ferrero) labels, c. 1930, influenced by the Art Deco style.

BEER

Quite early in the last century the beer trade in Britain was encouraged by two events: in 1830 beer duty was repealed (although the duty on malt was increased); and in 1834 the duty on glass was abolished. Up to this time customers had brought their own bottles to be filled, but now the brewers could afford to bottle their own beers.

As trade increased, it became necessary to find a more efficient way of marking a bottle with the brewer's name and the bottle's contents (this had been done previously by means of wax seals). Printed labels were the answer, and these were first used in the early 1840s. They were printed in black and white in a circular format (both Guinness and Bass originally used such labels). By the 1880s most labels had changed to an oval shape.

Right and **opposite** Beer labels of 1890-1930 with a bottle of Artist's Ale, c. 1965. The label for Bass pale ale was designed in 1855, an image familiar around the world. At one time, brewers must have been worried that unscrupulous people were refilling the empties, because during the 1880s, Whitbread labels carried the request "when empty please destroy the label."

GUINNESS

Guinness was first brewed in 1799. Circular labels were used from around 1840 (see central panel of label immediate left)

Left to **right** Bottler's own design, c.1890; label dated 19.9.99; design change, 1975; date code, 1983. The classic Guinness label was designed in 1862.

Below Commemorative labels were issued for Queen Victoria's Jubilees of 1887 and 1897, and in 1902 Bass made a special brew for Edward VII's Coronation, many bottles of which still survive, mostly unopened. Apart from royal events, which brewers have frequently commemorated during the past 35 years, other occasions have been celebrated by the issue of a beer with a special label. Benskin's, for instance, created a special brew when Watford reached the Cup Final in 1984.

SPA WATER

From the seventeenth century the mineral springs of Europe were centers where the gentry might "take the waters," both bathing in and drinking them for their healing properties. The most famous centers were Spa in Belgium, Evian, Perrier and Vichy in France, and Cheltenham and Malvern in England. The waters from these springs began to be bottled and distributed on a large scale during the nineteenth century.

Below As with so many other products, labels for spa waters began to appear in the 1850s. At first they were printed in black on a white background, but by the end of the 19th century muted colors were in use.

SOFT DRINKS AND SQUASHES

During the 1780s, the efforts of an "amateur scientist" called Jacob Schweppe, in collaboration with an expert in pumping machinery, resulted in the production of artificially produced mineral waters which were sold in Geneva. In 1792 Schweppe moved to London where he set up a mineral water factory.

The commercial production of cordials and squashes was established by the middle of the nineteenth century when companies, such as L. Rose & Co., bottled fruit juices, mainly lime or lemon. These were favored as medicinal drinks, particularly for the relief of rheumatism. By the end of the Victorian era, such drinks were commonly drunk in the form of effervescent refreshments.

Right The most successful types of stoppers for mineral waters over the past 150 years have been as follows: the Hamilton, from 1814 until the 1920s, the bottle being stored on its side to keep the cork moist; the internal screw, from 1872 until the 1950s; the swing stopper, from 1875 until the 1950s; the Codd, from 1875 until the 1920s, in which gas pressure kept a marble tight against a rubber ring; and the Crown cap, instituted in 1892 and still in use today (see the Perrier label illustrated on page 65). In the 1950s the external screw cap was developed, and this is today the most widely used stopper.

Left The labels for cordials and squashes, unlike those for bottled spa waters, were often brightly colored **Below** A feature of the long, elegant squash or cordial bottle was the embossed glass pattern. Rose's, with their lime-juice cordial, were probably the first to use such elaborate molded decorations, and they had many imitators. The bottles illustrated here date from c. 1900 (Rose's) to c. 1930 (Schweppes).

COFFEE

The social meeting place of the late seventeenth century was the coffee house, where coffee beans were roasted, ground and brewed on site. When the vogue for coffee houses declined from the 1730s onward (many were turned into ale houses), it was only the wealthy who continued to drink coffee. However, its popularity returned in the 1850s, as prices became more tolerable. French coffee, which was blended with chicory to make it cheaper, became a favored drink.

By the 1870s a number of manufacturers were packaging their own brands of coffee in cans. By the 1890s, Thomas Lipton led the field – mainly because he owned 400 retail outlets.

Colored labels were used to distinguish between different strengths of coffee and also to indicate their prices. The Lipton's labels date from c. 1885 (**above right**) and c. 1905 (**right**).

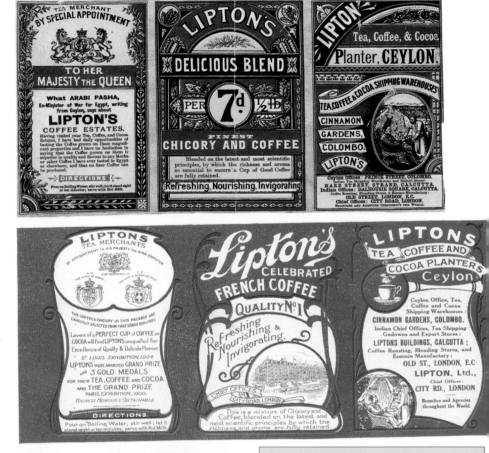

The arrival of "instant" coffee completely changed the market. Nestlé's Nescafé was launched in 1939; Maxwell House arrived in the UK in 1954.

Left Coffee essence in bottles was being sold as early as the 1850s, but it was the arrival of Camp coffee (which contained chicory) in 1885 that eventually made sales of essence higher than those of ground coffee. The Glasgow-based firm of R. Patterson manufactured Camp for the use of the Gordon Highlanders serving in India. By the 1930s the firm's expenditure on advertising Camp was equivalent to about 80 percent of that spent on all other brands of coffee combined. Until the late 1930s Camp, like most bottled coffee essences, was individually boxed. In 1957 the tray held by the label's Indian servant was removed, and in 1978 there was a complete update.

TEA AND HEALTH DRINKS

It is thought that tea was first drunk in China around 2,700BC. It took some time to reach Europe, first coming to the attention of Samuel Pepys on September 25, 1660, when he ''did send for a cup of tee, a China drink of which I never had drunk before.'' The drinking of tea became popular during the eighteenth century, and in the 1840s the first tea was grown in India. It was not only refreshing, it had stimulating qualities and was thought, like many other products, to aid digestion.

HORLICKS AND OVALTINE

Along with tea, cocoa and chocolate, a new type of health drink based on malt arrived at the beginning of this century. J. & W. Horlick, British emigrants to the United States, patented their malted milk in 1883, manufacturing it first in Chicago and then expanding production to Slough, England, in 1906. Ovaltine, formulated by a Swiss chemist, was first sold in 1904. It rapidly became popular throughout Europe. The British Ovaltine company was formed in 1909, and a factory built at Kings Langley four years later.

Right Horlicks and Ovaltine with their overwraps, c. 1935 **Left** Packaged tea blends from the CWS, c. 1935.

COCOA

Cocoa was first brought from the West Indies to Europe in the seventeenth century by the Portuguese, although it was the Dutch who became the most adept at manufacturing it. The English experimented with cocoa, but it was not until the duty on cocoa was reduced in 1832 that they began drinking cocoa in earnest.

Below In 1866, Cadbury became the first British company to produce a pure, concentrated cocoa – Cadbury's cocoa essence. Fry's version was launched two years later, and in 1880 Rowntree's Elect cocoa arrived. A Dutchman called Van Houten had formulated a pure cocoa as far back as 1828, and by 1900 the company he had founded was exporting a new "spicier" cocoa for which there was considerable demand. This prompted Cadbury, in 1906, to launch its Bourneville cocoa, which soon outsold Cadbury's own cocoa essence.

SWEET APPEAL

CONFECTIONERY · CHOCOLATE
· COOKIES · CAKES

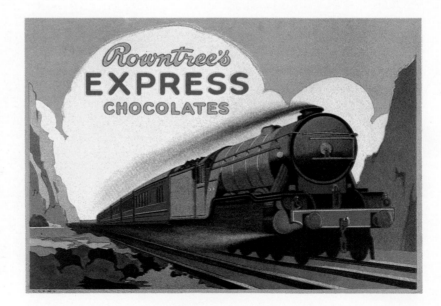

Outer box label, c. 1930.

CONFECTIONERY

In the early days most confectionery was sold by weighing out the quantity required for each customer, either from glass jars or wooden boxes. Some candies were made up into sticks or bars, and were sold individually, although they did not have their own wrappers. It was not until the 1860s that the packaging of confectionery in individual boxes began, for such delicacies as *fruit confits* and chocolate creams.

Up to the 1930s corner candy stores always had their rows of standard 5lb confectionery jars from which all manner of delights appeared, from velvet cushions to lemon sherbets, and even today some stores sell candy in this way. But shopping habits have changed and the glass (or, latterly, plastic) jar has largely been replaced by the pre-weighed plastic bag, and an array of boxes.

Top Two confectionery labels, c.1905 **Right** Cachou jars dating from c.1920. Barker & Dobson continued to use their design until the 1960s.

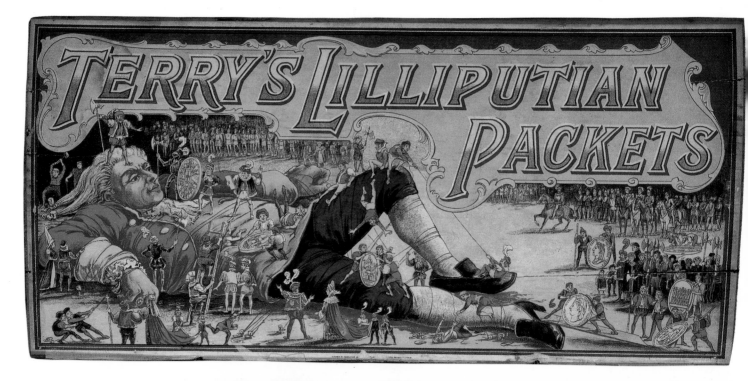

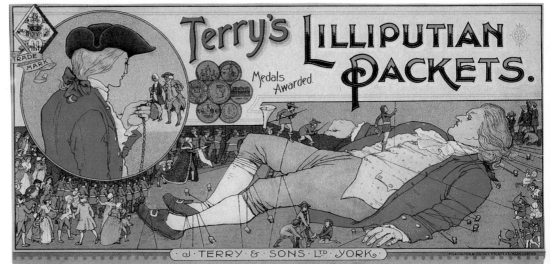

Inside lid labels from Terry's Lilliputian packets, c. 1885 (**above**) and c. 1890 (**right**).

CONFECTIONERY DISPLAY BOXES

It was probably in the 1860s that small wooden crates were first adapted for use as display units on shop counters. A colorful label was pasted inside the lid, and another was displayed on the front of the box. When the lid was lifted, the goods could be displayed enticingly on the grocer's counter, rather as if they were on a peddler's tray. Starch, metal polish, baking powder and mustard were customarily displayed in such units, but it was the confectionery manufacturers who made most use of them and continued to do so until the 1940s (by which time the boxes were made of cardboard rather than wood).

Designers of display-box labels had a wide expanse of paper with which to attract the customer's eye. As with advertisements, some styles were purely typographic and others pictorial. These boxes date from 1890 to 1920. (See also the Rowntree Express label illustrated on page 72.)

CHOCOLATE

The Spaniards introduced the custom of drinking chocolate to Europe around 1630. Almost a century later, in 1729, George II granted Letters Patent to Walter Churchman of Bristol, who had perfected a process for making drinking chocolate. These rights were acquired by Joseph Fry in 1761. Later, John Cadbury, who started his career in 1824 as a tea dealer and coffee roaster in Birmingham, also sold cocoa and chocolate, but he did not begin to manufacture these products until 1831. It was only in the 1840s that chocolate became available in an edible form .

Right and **below** Pictorial chocolate boxes from the 1880s and 1890s.

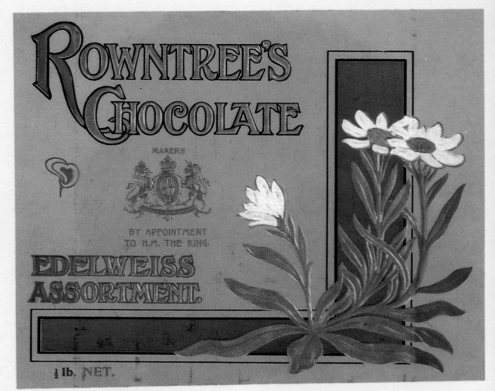

In 1868 both Fry and Cadbury introduced a novelty – the fancy chocolate box. These boxes had pictorial lids but no mention of the manufacturer's brand name was evident on the outside. At the time, there were few suitable colored picture labels in the printers' stocks, so Richard Cadbury decided to design his own. His first, a picture of a six-year-old girl, was printed by Goodall & Co. Inside was a discreet but carefully designed label giving the manufacturer's name.

Right Rowntree's chocolate box label, c.1905 **Below** Pictorial chocolate boxes from the 1880s and 1890s.

COOKIES

The popularity of cookies started during the eighteenth century when, in the British Navy, sailors were given ship's cookies as part of their rations. They were supplied in tin-lined wooden containers. These cookies were also used as provisions on military expeditions, and by explorers. By the 1840s fancy cookies began to be produced by Carr's of Carlisle, Meredith & Drew of London, and Huntley & Palmer's of Reading; within a decade they were being exported to the Continent and then to the rest of the world.

Labels have been designed to fit many shapes of biscuit tin. **Opposite page** The Huntley & Palmer's label (**below**) was created in 1876 and had changed little by the 1950s. The tin and label were covered by a transparent protective wrapping sealed by end labels **Right** Label for Amery Oliver biscuits, c.1890 **Far right** Label for Macfarlane Lang water biscuits, c.1930.

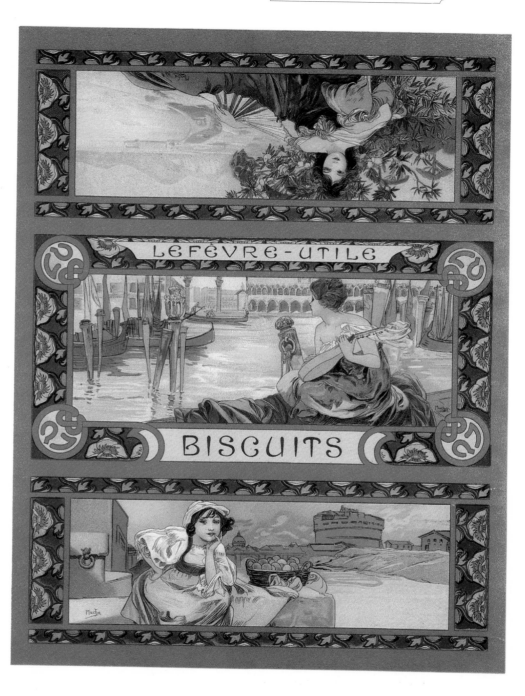

The firm of Lefevre-Utile had its origins in 1846, when the family set up as pastrycooks in Nantes, France. Louis Lefevre-Utile took over in 1883 and promptly expanded the business, setting up a factory and employing famous artists to advertise his cookies. The labels, too, were illustrated by artists in vogue; especially favored was Alphonse Mucha (1860-1939), the celebrated Czech painter and noted exponent of Art Nouveau.

The labels illustrated here date from c. 1900 (**left**) and c. 1910 (**above**).

Below For almost 100 years the stack of square tins labeled with the maker's name, each containing 8-9lbs of carefully packed cookies, was a familiar sight in any grocery store. Even as late as 1939 most British cookies were sold "loose," weighed out from these tins. However, the emergence of the self-service store in the 1950s soon ended the artform of labels for large cookie tins **Right** Labels dating from 1905, although the designs for Breakfast and Tiffin were actually created in the 1850s and 1880s, respectively **Opposite page** CWS cookie label, c.1900.

C.W.S.

PINEAPPLE

Biscuits

Crumpsall Works, MANCHESTER.

PEEK FREAN'S
PEEK, FREAN & Co., Ltd.
BISCUIT MANUFACTURERS,
LONDON: ENGLAND.
PRINTED IN GREAT BRITAIN

A selection of cookie-tin labels from the 1930s – except Huntley and Palmer's chocolate dessert, c. 1915.
Opposite page Peek Frean label from c. 1925.

CAKES

Many cookie manufacturers included the production of both plain and fancy cakes in their range, especially for the Christmas trade. As early as 1840 Huntley & Palmer's was selling four kinds of cake as well as the seasonal Twelfth Night Cake and Rich Bride Cake (made to order). By the 1870s some cakes were being wrapped with printed bands around their middle, or packed in white boxes with colorful round labels on the lid and often a small, single-color label inside.

Cake-box labels, c. 1905.

Macfarlane Lang cake-box labels, c. 1930. Usually cake boxes were made of white cardboard with the label stuck on the top of the lid. Possibly for display purposes, a more solid box was sometimes provided with an inner glass lid and an interior label. This was the case with the Broadcast cake . . . aptly tuned in to the newly popular wireless.

FOOD FOR ALL SEASONS

MEAT EXTRACTS · OILS, VINEGARS AND SAUCES
· CHEESE · JAMS AND MARMALADES · MUSTARD
· CANNED FOODS · DATES · FRESH FRUIT

Detail from showcard, c. 1915.

MEAT EXTRACTS

During the 1840s in Germany, Baron Justus von Liebig perfected a concentrated meat extract. By the 1890s sales had reached eight million jars a year. A reformulated extract named Oxo was launched in 1900, which eventually replaced Liebig's Extract (or Lemco as it was renamed to avoid confusion with its many imitators). Another meat extract, Bovril, was first sold in Canada in 1874 under the name of its inventor John Johnston, a Scotsman. After a fire at his factory he moved to London, and Bovril went on sale in 1886, using the distinctive squat bottles with red labels.

Below Meat extracts, c. 1910.

Left Liebig jar, c. 1890
Many other brands were also appearing at this time: Borthwick's fluid beef, Hipi mutton essence, Bonovin's Exox, CWS Silvox, Foster Clark's Ju-Vis, Viskor, Verox, Beefex, Vimbos, Vigoral, and Hugon's Torox. Most imitated Bovril and used labels with red backgrounds. The exceptions were Valentine's meat juice and Armour's beef juice, both American products.

Bovril jars of c. 1905 and 1987, and Marmite jars of c. 1935 and 1987.

OILS, VINEGARS AND SAUCES

Since Roman times the use of oils and spices as a means of enlivening food has been part of culinary art. Spices became more varied after 1500, when the spice routes between the Orient and Western Europe were opened up. A hundred years later the British East India Company was formed, and by 1800 it had brought to England every type of pickle, sauce, spice and vinegar, although they could be afforded only by the well-to-do. However, it was not long before many concoctions produced commercially in Britain were on the market. The firm of John Burgess, established in 1760, and known for its essence of anchovies, produced an oyster sauce and Mogul sauce (an early brand name) in the 1820s. A fishmonger in Reading, James Cocks, had invented a sauce in 1802 that was soon sold throughout Britain.

In 1823 Lea & Perrins set up business in Worcester as chemists and druggists. By chance they were able to acquire a recipe for a sauce that had originated in Bengal, and Lea & Perrins' Worcestershire Sauce was first sold in 1837. Like them, Crosse & Blackwell (formed in 1830) began producing foodstuffs which they soon extended to malt vinegar and mixed relishes.

Above and **opposite** Bottles from the period 1890-1940. The Lazenby's Harvey's sauce label is still in the style of the 1830s

Above Two of the most famous sauces – HP and Daddies – were introduced by the Midland Vinegar Company (founded 1875), and arrived comparatively late: HP sauce was relaunched in 1903, and in the same year Daddies sauce was registered as a brand name, sales commencing soon after. The recipes for these sauces were acquired in 1899 from Frederick Garton, who had recorded the secret recipe for HP Sauce in his 1894 diary and who had presumably made the sauce from that year onward.

CHEESE

Individual farmers were responsible for the production of local cheese up until the nineteenth century, when the cheese factory started to establish itself. In Europe there was little cheese produced on farms after 1920. Cheese labels probably began to appear at the end of the nineteenth century as a colorful addition to the identification marks on the rind and on wooden boxes. When processed cheese became popular during the 1920s, the variety of cheese flavors increased and along with them the enormous variety of label designs.

The labels on this page date from 1890 (**left**) to about 1910 (**above** and **right**). The labels shown **opposite** are from the 1930s.

JAMS AND MARMALADES

For generations, households have made their own jams and marmalades, and bottled their own fruits. It was therefore understandable that the public viewed "store-made" jam with certain reservations, and for many this prejudice lasted until the disappearance of the domestic servant. The popularity of marmalade, made mainly from oranges grown in Seville, grew during the fifteenth century. The Scots were particularly fond of it, and many stores sold their own produce.

James Keiller started selling marmalade in 1797; it was not until 1864 that James Robertson did so also. At this time, stoneware jars were used with designs in black being transferred directly onto the surface. Colored paper labels were in use on stoneware and glass jars by the 1890s. Robertson's adopted the golly as their trademark in 1914 and, since 1928, the paper golly has been stuck to the jars. It is interesting to see how the Robertson's marmalade label has changed in emphasis to Golden Shred.

Left and **below** Jam jars, 1905-1935. The Robertson's jars (**opposite**) date from (left to right) c. 1895, c. 1925, c. 1935 and 1987. The advertisement showing the overwrapped jar was painted by A. H. Sands, c. 1925.

MUSTARD

The first mustard-producing company to flourish was that of Messrs. Keen, who set up their mustard factory in London in 1742. The story of Colman's mustard began in 1814 when Jeremiah Colman moved his milling business to an existing flour and mustard mill near Norwich. The bull's head trademark has been used by Colman's since 1855. Most mustard during the nineteenth century was distributed in oak casks which, from the 1850s, bore round labels for identification. It was at the same time that mustard tins first appeared with labels.

Below left Three of the many changes in the Colman's mustard label over the years **Below** The traditional design, this particular example dating from c. 1905 **Below right** The 1975 update with the bull's head having been removed. 1980 brought a return to "Victorian values," but with a new-look bull's head.

Left A curious feature of the penny oval label was the color combination of red, blue and black. The stripes allowed for six possible variants to be used at the same time, for no apparent reason.

Yellow was the obvious basic color to use for mustard labels. The design for Keen's (**above**) probably dated from the 1860s, with the medals being added later. (The item shown is a folding pocket calendar of 1901.) The design of the Champion's label (**below left**) is more akin to the designs of the 1870s. The £1,000 reward was probably added in the 1880s, when Lever was making a similar announcement on his Sunlight soap boxes.

CANNED FOODS

The first company to produce canned foods on a commercial scale was Donkin and Hall, in 1812. They found glass too fragile and corks too porous, so they began to use soldered tinplate containers for their food. The British Navy was among its first customers, and much praise was received for these tins from Arctic explorers. By 1830 canned goods began to appear in shops.

During the next hundred years canned foods were often frowned upon as being either a poor substitute for the fresh equivalent or a lazy way to prepare a meal. Nevertheless, in her book on household management, Mrs. Beeton commented that "tinned food is a valuable substitute for salt meat on board ship and elsewhere, and is especially useful to persons removed from the general source of supply."

In America, metal canisters were used after 1837 when glass jars became too expensive. During the Civil War cans were used extensively and this hastened their acceptance in the home. By the 1880s canning factories for all types of foods had spread across America.

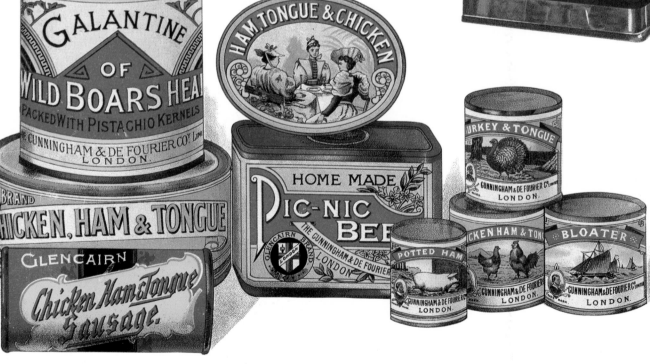

Opposite page Details from showcards, c. 1900 Below US fruit and vegetable cans, c. 1900.

Top The label of Fait & Winebrenner of Baltimore dates from the early 1870s. The girl is shown holding a tomato can on whose label she appears **Center** and **below** Both the French label for Tunis tomato paste and the Spanish tomato label date from 1910-20.

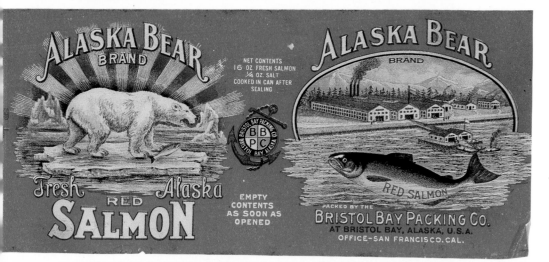

Each year, during the months of April, May and June, the salmon caught off the coasts of Alaska and British Columbia were packed into cans by hand. The label for Alaska Bear salmon shows the packing station at Bristol Bay, one of many along the coast. Canned salmon tasted much the same whichever company produced it, and so the label played a fundamental role in persuading the retailer or customer to buy one product rather than another. Innumerable brand-names were created, each illustrated appropriately on the label: Moose Queen, Frost King, Ocean Spray, Jack Frost, Silver Net, Arctic Red, Cherokee, North Pole and Coral Queen. If all else failed, the manufacturer might resort to a play on words, such as Soo-Pere-Yor and Red-E-Lunch (the latter because canned salmon was quite cheap until the outbreak of World War II.) Here are labels used by Ocean Brand and Home Brand, c.1890, and by Alaska Bear and Jap, c.1900.

DATES

During the middle of the nineteenth century, dried fruits such as Muscatel raisins from Malaga, in Spain, and dates from North Africa, were arriving in small wooden boxes with pictorial labels. (John Yeats, in *The Natural History of Commerce*, 1870, said that the best dates came from Tunis, via Marseilles.) By the 1890s the now traditional oblong box with rounded ends had been developed, with its romantic label depicting date-laden palm trees, camels, and grand harbors. The heyday of these boxes has now passed; many are now made of plastic, with even a plastic imitation stem lying between the rows of fruit, instead of a real one.

Date-box labels of the 1890s, and a label for Kitty Brand (one of the more lasting makes), c. 1900.

Date-box labels from the 1930s. To go with the exotic pictures, date-box labels had appropriate brand-names: Jericho, Rainbow, Silhouette, Tropic, Orient, Oasis Star, Mustang and Echo-o-o; in the 1950s a popular brand was Eat Me. The initials "BOB" stood for "best of brands."

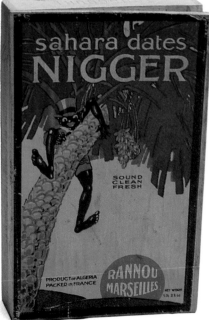

FRESH FRUIT

The climate of California is ideal for growing fruit; by the 1870s a flourishing trade was developing there, particularly in oranges. During the next twenty years many settlers came to cultivate this promised land and a vast complex of fruit-growers developed. Oranges were packed in wooden crates, and in order to identify the orchard from which they came, branded pictorial labels were pasted to either end.

Many of the early labels were taken from stock designs held by the printers in San Francisco. These labels depicted images such as a bowl of fruit, an orchard scene or a beautiful señorita feeding doves. Having chosen the image, a suitable brand name of the grower's choice could then be added to the label. However, as time went on the same picture was often chosen by a dozen different growers, which caused confusion in the market, because it is the pictorial image which attracts the eye rather than a brand name. The remedy for this situation was to make labels specifically for each individual fruit-grower.

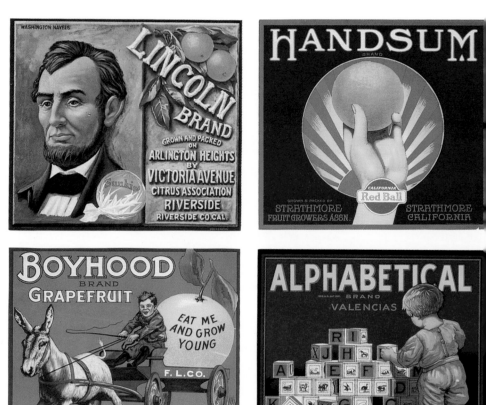

John Salkin and Laurie Gordon describe in their book *Orange Crate Art* how one enterprising printer carried a caseful of stock vignettes, pictures of fruit in various states of unpeel, competitors' labels, magazine clippings and postcards, when visiting fruit-growers. From this mixture he was able to create a unique label, working with scissors and paste, perhaps also using a photograph of the grower's wife or a sketch of their ranch home.

Above and **opposite page** Orange crate labels: Boyhood, c. 1915; Lincoln, c. 1925; Alphabetical and California Dream, 1928; Handsum, 1935 **Left** The label on the crate of Blue Mountain brand Jamaica oranges, some of which are individually wrapped, dates from the 1890s.

By 1900, 500 or so different orange brand names were in use in California. By 1930 this figure had increased to about 2,000. Some growers, however, went out of business. The sharp practice grew up whereby successful growers would buy up defunct labels and use them to market a poor season's crop, so that they did not risk jeopardizing their own reputation.

A contrast in fashions — FB apples, c. 1910, and melon labels of the 1940s.

LIGHTING UP

PIPE TOBACCO · CIGARETTES
· CIGARS · MATCHES

German cigar label, c. 1910.

PIPE TOBACCO

During the 1590s and after, the port of Bristol was well situated to receive the growing imports of tobacco leaf from America, and was second only to the port of London. (Two hundred years later Liverpool and Glasgow took a share of these imports.) Around these ports, numerous cottage industries which processed tobacco grew up (for instance, by 1881 there were 570 licensed tobacco manufacturers).

During the 1860s tin boxes were used for larger quantities of tobacco, and had labels pasted on them. As color printing improved, so labels became more colorful and helped to glamorize the tobacco brands. By the 1890s many tins had the image printed directly onto the surface of the tin, thus improving the quality of the overall image; paper was, after all, subject to being torn or scuffed.

Tobacco tins, c. 1900. The labels were often stuck inside the lid as well as on the top.

CIGARETTES

In 1890 cigarettes accounted for less than half of one percent of tobacco sales but within 10 years they made up 12 percent of the market. This massive increase was due almost entirely to the introduction of the Bonsack cigarette machine in 1884; a new era had begun — that of cheap cigarettes such as Woodbine, launched in 1888.

Airtight tins for tobacco and cigarettes, dating from the period 1880-1920. The development of a built-in cutter removed the risk of damaging cigarettes while opening the tin; in the past a can-opener had been necessary. In the opened Player's Navy Cut tin we can see the 50 cigarettes as well as the paper tag used to help pull out the first few.

During the 1860s tin boxes were used for larger quantities of tobacco, and had labels pasted on them. As color printing improved, so labels became more colorful and helped to glamorize the tobacco brands. By the 1890s many tins had the image printed directly onto the surface of the tin, thus improving the quality of the overall image; paper was, after all, subject to being torn or scuffed.

CIGARS

Cigars are known to have been smoked in the tenth century, and Columbus found them in Cuba and South America, introducing them to Spain around 1700. Smoking cigars was then, and still is today, seen as a symbol of wealth. It was natural, therefore, that the boxes they were sold in should look opulent. Richly decorated labels, often embossed, appeared all over the boxes – on the lid, as a seal around the box and under the lid. This tradition has hardly changed in more than a hundred years.

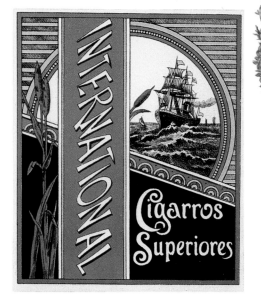

Top The First Rate cigar label was printed during the 1870s for the London tobacco manufacturer Redford & Co. The design was registered by the company as a trademark. Contrasting styles: **Above** A label from the 1890s, traditional for Havana cigars – highly decorated and embossed, superbly printed, with gold medals and full of detail and romance. Labels much like this are still in use today **Left** the modern style, c. 1900 (and see also page 106).

ARTHUR DONALDSON

AS PRINCE OF PILSEN

I know no greater pleasure
Mid the trials that hedge the day
Than to light a good Havana
And to smoke my cares away

MAKER F.C. LUNDQUIST CHICAGO.

PILSEN

F.C. LUNDQUIST
MANUFACTURER OF HAVANA CIGARS
CHICAGO

Despite its long tradition, cigar consumption has always been a small part of the tobacco market. In Britain they became more popular during the 1840s, yet amounted to only two percent of tobacco sales. By 1880 there were about 300 small cigar-making establishments, mainly in London, which accounted for two-thirds of cigar production. The rest were imported chiefly from Havana, although American cigars, mainly from New York, began to replace the cheaper sorts from Cuba in the 1880s and 1890s, as the popularity of cigar-smoking increased.

The making of cigars was a labor-intensive job, but in the 1930s machine-made cigars, such as Wills Whiffs, started to appear. The art of hand-rolling cigars is still necessary for the larger cigars today.

Left Display card for Arthur Donaldson cigars, c. 1910. Each cigar has a paper band bearing a motif **Below** Ye Black Friars cigar box, c. 1900.

MATCHES

Friction matches were first available in 1827. By the 1850s they had become commonplace, and were available in wooden, cardboard or tin containers. At this time most matches were manufactured in Germany, Austria, Sweden and Britain. Bryant & May, provision merchants in London, began by importing Swedish matches which were sold under its name in 1851. In 1861 the company started to manufacture its own safety matches as well.

Like most other labels in the 1850s, those for matches were plain (see page 10) although some used single colors. It was in the 1860s and 1870s that the multi-colored matchbox labels with bold, pictorial designs came into being.

Right Bryant & May matches and almanac for 1875. Swan White Pine Vestas were introduced in 1897 with a design similar to this one (c.1915); in 1959 the box was redesigned and the swan was at last allowed to swim toward the center of the image instead of heading out of it. Their cigar lights became "braided" to prevent the heads dropping off.
Right The Runaway match, showing two match sticks eloping from the box, was issued in 1871.

Left British matchboxes, 1880-1920. The front and back of the Conquering Hero box is shown. On the backs of the Salmon & Gluckstein boxes (**bottom left**), a number of different designs were used incorporating a penny coin dated for that year – 1898, 1905, 1911 and 1916 **Below** The Football match label, c.1885, is unusual in that it hardly makes the user aware either of its manufacturer or its brand name.

The matchbox labels illustrated on this page and opposite (1895-1935) come from around the world, particularly from Sweden — the home of the match. No other category of label shows such incredible variety of design or wide choice of subject. A popular theme was the "threesome": Three Monkeys, Three Birds, Three Stars and Three Poodles. The swastika was at one time a symbol of luck.

Many notable people have collected matchbox labels, including royalty. One was King Chulaongkorn of Siam (who incidentally collected wives as well – eighty-two in all). During a visit to London in 1897, he once astonished his entourage by darting forward to retrieve an unusual matchbox he had spied in the gutter of Oxford Street.

HOME AND AWAY

DISINFECTANT · POLISH AND VARNISH · STARCH
· INK AND GLUE · STATIONERY · LUGGAGE
· FIREWORKS AND CRACKERS · GAMES · CLOTHES
· CLOTH BALES · TWINE

Hotel luggage label, c. 1925.

DISINFECTANT AND BLEACH

In the 1870s Joseph Lister became aware of the dangers of bacteria and began to draw the public's attention to the risk. During the next 20 years public demand created a market for disinfectants. John Jeyes developed a disinfectant fluid in 1877, selling it to those living around Plaistow, Essex, which happened to be near Joseph Lister's birthplace. In 1883 Izal was launched having been sold previously as Thorncliffe Patent disinfectant. In the next year Lever's Lifebuoy soap arrived, a carbolic soap containing a germicide.

Below Disinfectant bottles of the 1950s. Pine was a popular aroma of freshness, the image being reflected in some designs.

Below Izal, c.1900; ammonia bottles, c.1920; Brobat, c.1950, but the label was designed in the 1920s.

POLISH AND VARNISH

The Industrial Revolution brought a wave of change. Factories sprang up billowing smoke, towns grew rapidly to house the factory-workers and dust and dirt was everywhere. Fortunately, among the flow of new products were a range of floor and furniture polishes or varnishes to keep indoor surfaces sparkling. The labels for household products fell into two main categories; those that relied on a typographic design and those that used a pictorial image, often of the product itself.

Below These products of 1885–1925 have a range of label styles — script only for Meltonian with a green background, the pictorial trade mark of the Chelsea Pensioner, the factory scene on Adams' composition, and others showing the product in use.

KNIFE POLISH

Before the advent of stainless
steel cutlery in the 1930s, the
correct way to clean knives
was to use a knife-cleaning
machine or an India-rubber and
buff leather knife-board in
conjunction with the right
amount of knife polish. This
polish consisted of finely
ground emery, which was
sprinkled from canisters with
perforated tops. John Oakey &
Sons was a leading maker of
this polish (1850s-1940s) and
produced many other domestic
requisites under its Wellington
brand name, including black
lead, furniture cream, plate
powder and silversmith soap.

Below Knife polish canisters,
1880-1920. The design of Oakey's
Wellington polish label probably
dates from the 1850s. It remained
unchanged with the exception
that Wellington's profile changed
from right to left. Originally the
label had a green background, but
later blue and red backgrounds
were introduced.

STARCH

Part of the Victorian wash-day ritual was the starching of clothes. According to *Mrs Beeton's Book of Household Management* it was "a process by which stiffness is communicated to certain parts of linen, as the collars and fronts of shirts."

By 1900 the starch market was dominated by two companies: J. & J. Colman (who took over Orlando Jones and Co. in 1901), and Reckitt and Sons Ltd, who merged with Colman's in 1938. Today Reckitt's Robin starch, which was launched in 1899, is the sole survivor.

Left Colman's starch label, c. 1900
Below Starch boxes c. 1920. When compared to the special pictorial labels produced for children's scrap books (see page 24), these labels are straightforward and dignified.

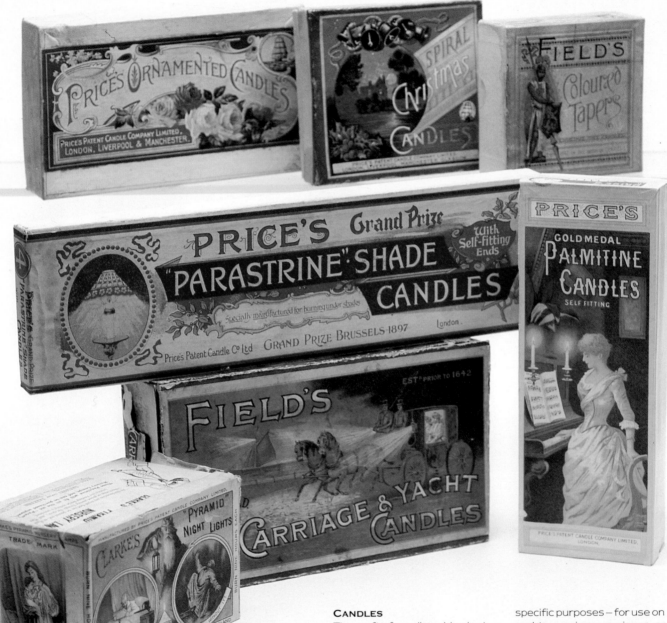

CANDLES

The craft of candlemaking is at least 2,000 years old. Until the 19th century it was a cottage industry, but then candles started to be manufactured for specific purposes — for use on yachts, carriages or pianos, or as nightlights. Price's (founded 1830) made piano candles from 1880, renaming them Palmitine candles in 1982.

INK AND GLUE

Both ink and glue were known to early civilizations. The Egyptians used glue in woodworking around 3300 BC and flour paste for the production of papyrus. Inks of various types were known to have been in use by 2500 BC by both the Egyptians and the Chinese.

As the art of writing developed, by the 1840s ready-made liquid inks were more popular than the powdered form that required mixing with water. Small glass bottles of ink were decorated with delicate single color labels. For the larger quantities of ink stoneware jars were produced which had more decorative labels. Ink manufacturers often extended their product range to include glue, but it was the specifically developed brands like Gloy that dominated the market.

Below Standard ink label, c. 1880.

Ink bottles of c. 1900. The labels of Lyon's and Stephen's ink use a style influenced by the designs of lottery tickets (abolished in 1826) and bank notes.

Ink bottles of the 1920s and 1930s. Glass bottles were now used for large quantities of ink.

Below Selection of glue bottles. The Gloy label of the 1930s contrasts sharply with the 1880s design of Judson and Le Page labels.

STATIONERY

The street peddler of the eighteenth century traveled from one village to the next selling boxes, ribbon, chapbooks and writing materials. When the towns began to grow, the peddler could afford to sell his wares from a fixed site and thus became "stationary." During the early years of the nineteenth century a vast range of stationery was being packaged — writing paper, sealing wax, quill pens, metal pen nibs, and even wafers for sealing envelopes.

Below right Stationery boxes, c. 1910 **Right** Directional label, c. 1930 **Below** The "Don't Crush" labels come from the days when the railways were widely used to send all sorts of things, no matter how fragile.

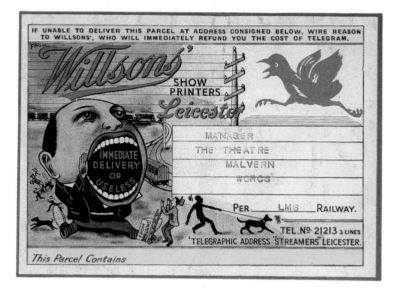

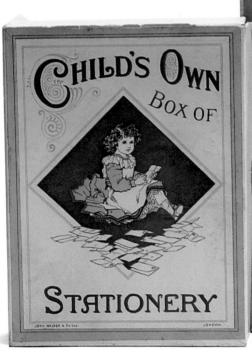

PEN NIBS

By 1850 metal pen nibs had virtually replaced the quill pen. John Mitchell of Birmingham is credited with the invention in 1828 of the machine-made steel point, which was soon followed by the improved pen of James Perry. Other manufacturers, such as George Hughes and Johnson Bros, both from Birmingham, were among a number of companies which issued boxes usually containing one gross of steel pens.

The quest for a successful ink pen with a continuous flow began in the seventeenth century. A satisfactory solution was finally reached by an American insurance salesman, L. E. Waterman, in 1884. By the time the first Biro ballpoint pen went on sale in 1945 (it had been invented in 1938), the use of the dip-and-write pen was on its way out.

Below Pen-nib boxes dating from the 1890s to the 1920s. A sample nib was often attached to the outside of the box at one end; Perry's Albert pen made a feature of this on the lid.

LUGGAGE

The art of the luggage label was most conspicuous during the 1920s and 1930s when Continental travel became more popular and yet still had a certain snob appeal. At this time overseas travel was by passenger liner, and it was not unusual for intrepid travelers to take ten trunks or cases with them. All baggage which arrived on board was labeled, and as well as bearing the passenger's name the label stated whether a particular piece of luggage was to be taken to the cabin or was "not required on voyage" (i.e. destined for the hold).

Hotels supplied their own labels in advance, which again helped to ensure that the luggage arrived at the correct destination, but was more often seen as a useful form of free advertising. On the other hand, for the status-seeker there was nothing better than a case plastered with prestigious hotel luggage labels. Today, the right shopping bag in one's hand, or designer label on one's clothes, is in much the same way a statement of superiority.

Right and **opposite page** Luggage labels from the 1920s and 1930s (except the Grand Hôtel de Saxe label of c. 1890 and the Hôtel du Ruth label of c. 1905). Some hotels used miniature forms of their posters; occasionally the same view was used by different hotels, as here of Bellagio.

FIREWORKS AND CRACKERS

Since the seventeenth century, many occasions of national rejoicing have been celebrated by displays of fireworks. Mr. Brock was organizing firework displays in 1816, and by the 1880s there were a number of other manufacturers such as Pain, Wilder, Wells and Harrison. It was probably during the early years of this century, when indoor fireworks became popular, that boxes containing a selection of bangers, whizzers and catherine wheels started to appear. The packaging of Christmas crackers must have begun a few decades earlier because by 1860 commercial production of crackers had started.

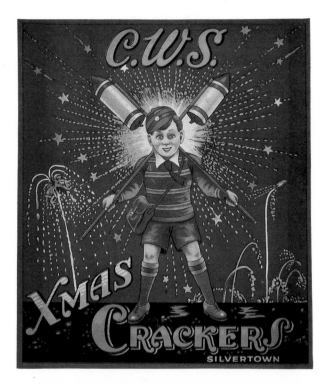

Top CWS cracker box, c. 1930
Above Wilder's fireworks box, c. 1935 **Left** Tom Smith's parlor fireworks box, c. 1910.

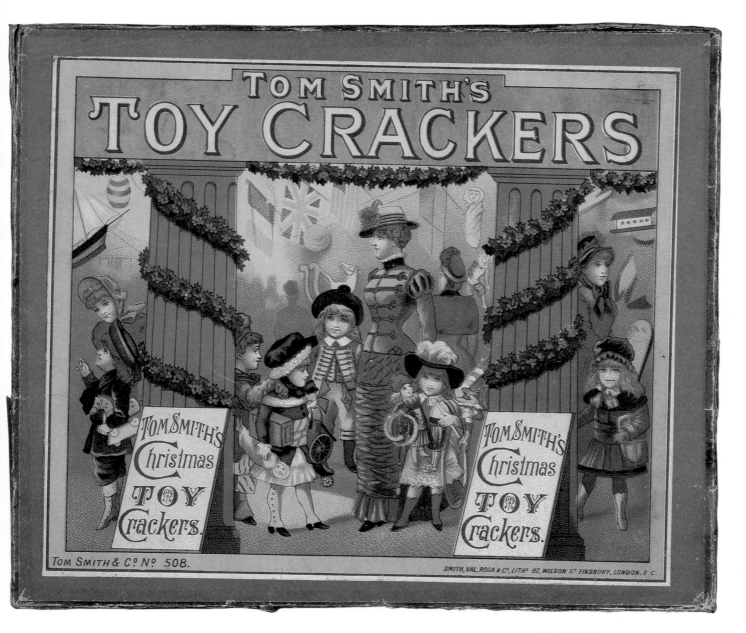

Tom Smith's toy cracker box, c. 1900.

GAMES

From the day in 1766 when the first jigsaw pieces were placed in a wooden box, a label was required to state its contents. Since then, the box lid label has become an essential part of selling boxed games, toys and puzzles. As the boxes grew in size so did their labels. In many instances, however, the label would oversell the product and when the lid was removed, disappointment would lie within.

In America, boxed board games were being produced in the 1840s. Monopoly – the invention of Charles Darrow, an unemployed engineer – arrived in 1935. The following year Britain was swept by the Monopoly craze.

Right Snakes & Ladders box, c.1900. A traditional game in India, it was patented in Britain in 1892
Below Boxed game, c.1910.

Above and **far left** Boxed toys
c. 1935 **Left** "How Silas Popped
the Question," US, c. 1915. In
1919, the *Daily Mirror* started a
comic strip featuring the
adventures of Pip, Squeak and
Wilfred. They became so
popular that boxed games,
jigsaws and even a handkerchief
painting outfit were produced.
Most notable of many other
children's characters was
Mickey Mouse who in the 1930s
built up a huge following around
the world.

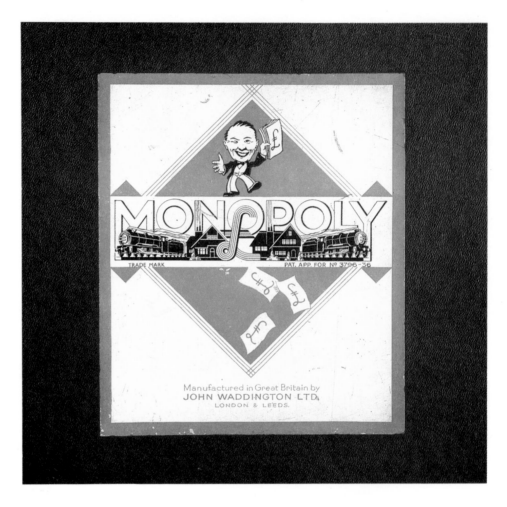

Contrasting styles of presentation. **Above** The carefully designed label for Monopoly (this is the British version which arrived in 1936) **Left** The label for the British Navy, crudely fashioned in Japan at the beginning of this century.

CLOTHES

As garment manufacturers started to advertise their wares nationally toward the end of the Victorian era, it became necessary and advantageous for some of them to box their creations. This was true especially of corsets, their need being popularized by the slim-waisted look of the day. Harness Electric corsets ("a boom to women of all ages"), for example, dispatched their corsets in boxes through the mail. The boxing of corsets gave the manufacturers a direct link with their customers, and directions printed on the box could not get lost. In addition, the image on the label could "promote" the goods inside the box.

Below Corset boxes, c. 1905
Below right Peter Pan socks and Emerald collar boxes, c. 1930.

CLOTH

Until the advent of man-made fibers, cotton had a great effect on the leading industrial nations, both politically and economically. In England the cotton industry played a great part in the Industrial Revolution and in employment; in the United States the cultivation of cotton has been established so long that it appears to be indigenous, which it is not. In 1900 the USA dominated the cotton supply in both quantity and quality, followed by India, Egypt and China.

Cotton cloth found a ready market in nearly every country of the world; Britain, for example, exported 90 percent of its cloth, primarily to India, Canada, Australia and the Far East. Trademarks for the thousands of different brands were added to all exported bales, either by means of a label, or by printing them directly onto the cloth. The labels were gummed to the paper in which the goods were packed and to the outermost fold of the piece of cloth.

Particularly in the case of India or China, where most merchants were illiterate, familiar images such as animals or soldiers were printed in color on the labels. These symbols became the means whereby the merchant recognized and distinguished the quality and type of cloth.

Cloth bale labels. **Top left** French, 1870s **Top right** British, 1870s **Bottom left** British, 1860s **Bottom right** British, 1890s. **Opposite** Chinese bale labels, c. 1900, attached to the cloth. The label or impression stamped directly on to the cotton shirting was known as a "chop" or trademark.

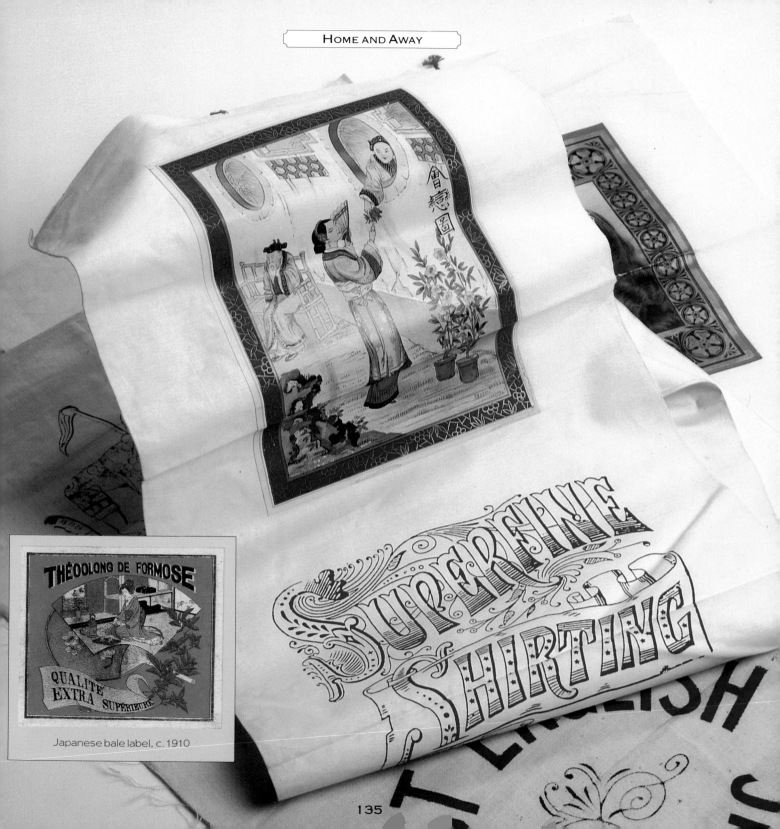

Japanese bale label, c. 1910

Right Bale labels or "tickets" for cloth exported from Britain to India, c.1890. Printed in Britain, these labels depicted Indian scenes, sometimes religious and occasionally grotesque, like the ceremonial disemboweling of a human body. They were drawn in a traditional Indian style.

Below right Bale labels of the 1920s. During this period a new style of bale label with bolder designs arrived replacing the intricate motifs of the Victorian era. Designs might be based on a variety of topics – portrayals of animals, famous people, events or monuments (the Skylon of the 1951 Festival of Britain was drawn on one).

Left Cotton bale labels designed for A.D. Steinthal & Co, US by E. McKnight Kauffer.

In the story of labels there are few which include the signature of the designer, and this is still the case today. It is only when the artist has a good reputation often in the world of poster art, that the signature becomes an asset to the label. This was the case with the cookie labels by Mucha (see page 79), the confectionery label (c. 1928) by the German artist Lucian Zabel (see page 1) and again here with these creations by McKnight Kauffer. In 1933, Cadbury's issued 11 chocolate boxes, each with a lid designed by an established artist, including Dame Laura Knight or Christopher Nevinson. However, the public did not take to these "strikingly different" box tops and the exercise was not repeated.

TWINE

In France during the second half of the nineteenth century, there was a flourishing twine trade, centered on the town of Lille. Originating from a cottage industry, some 140 twine manufacturers existed by the 1870s. Each company packed its twine in standard boxes, labeling them with a highly decorative, but distinctive design. The remarkable fact about these labels was that, almost without exception, the company names were abbreviated down to the initial letters. Thus A. Fanchille Delaroy was represented by the letters AFD.

Left, below and **opposite** French twine labels, c. 1875-1885. The printers of these labels were based in Paris or Lille where hundreds of different themes were created. The label (**left**) has a space at the base for the manufacturer's initials.

COLLECTING LABELS

It is said that 3,000 years ago Tutankhamun collected walking sticks. More recently it was the arrival of colorful, mass-produced, printed items that accelerated the popularity of collecting, making it more widespread and often compulsive. The prime example of collecting has been that of adhesive postage stamps, from the time they were first issued in 1840 (Stanley Gibbons started his trade in stamps in 1856) to the present day, when there are thought to be about 50 million collectors worldwide.

Whenever and wherever printed ephemera has been produced in sufficient quantities and in satisfac-

tory or uniform shapes, the collector has not been far behind – postcards, theater posters and cigarette cards (specifically produced to encourage loyalty to the brands that issued them) were all collected as they came out.

At the same time those who wanted to soak labels off cheese boxes, beer bottles or matchboxes could fill their scrapbooks with the ever-increasing wealth of designs being issued at home and abroad. Starch manufacturers in the 1890s and early 1900s produced series of pictorial labels on their boxes (see page 24), many of which found their way into children's scrapbooks along with other colored labels off tins, cans and boxes.

It seems that all manner of people became addicted to collecting labels; it is even said that in 1859 a royal couple searched Europe for rare matchbox labels.

Today, well-organized clubs and societies flourish, and the study of matchbox labels (phillumeny), beer labels (labology) or camembert cheese labels (tryroemiophily) is taken as seriously as philatelists take the study of postage stamps. Indeed, it is in theory possible to gather over 20,000 different British beer labels, and one collector has assembled over 125,000 beer labels from all over the world. It is quite common to find individuals who have amassed over 30,000 different matchbox labels, although the record

number, held by an American, is 280,000.

For the social historian, it is necessary to see labels in their environment, still attached to the box or bottle to which they were once stuck. In much the same way the postal historian who studies the postal service requires not just the stamp but the whole envelope with

Left Fletcher's sauce bottle, c.1920, unearthed from a garbage dump. **Above** Burgess label change, 1984 **Above opposite** Lea & Perrins label, 1980 **Below opposite** Corned beef can, c.1920. This can survived because it was used as a shelf support.

postmarks and any further documentation. To make a study of matches, therefore, the entire matchbox with its contents is needed together with the further surviving evidence of catalogs, advertisements and social references. However, for many collectors fun and satisfaction can be derived from acquiring the seemingly endless flat labels, either historic or modern, which can be neatly filed away in albums or mounted on display cards.

Another collecting craze developed during the mid-nineteenth century when multi-colored pot lids were produced for such diverse products as hair cream and meat paste. So attractive were they that they were purchased as much for the lids as their contents. These lids are still much sought after today, along with the many other items that can be dug out of Victorian and Edwardian garbage dumps such as pot lids

with black and white designs, glass bottles of different shapes and colors, and stone or pottery jars often with the manufacturer's inscription marked on the side.

What is not often appreciated from the bottles that are dug up, is that a huge proportion would originally have had labels on them, even though the manufacturer's name, address and the brand were embossed on the glass sides of the bottle. Just occasionally a partial label will survive being buried, such as appears on this Fletcher's Sauce bottle of around 1920 (far left). Here all that remains is the printed color; the paper itself has disintegrated.

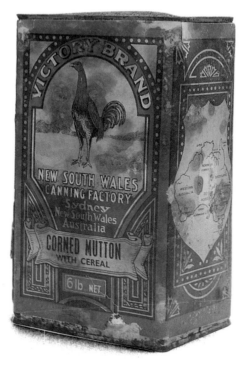

For those who wish to start collecting labels, there is an enormous range from which to choose. But it is not always easy to find the earlier labels unless you buy them from antique stores or fairs, collectors' markets, society meetings or at auctions. Early labels can, however, be found by chance in scrapbooks, on boxes used for storage in attics or cellars, or even at the back of the pantry of an elderly relative. During recent years, some labels have been found in large quantities, such as the American fruit crate labels (see pages 102-105), which are not only more readily available but are often in near-mint condition.

In many ways it is just as satisfying to save the labels which are currently in the corner store or supermarket, and if set about in the right way such a collection can make an interesting and useful social study. Even after a few years the designs will have changed, and there will have been countless offers and competitions added to the labels. New brands will have appeared, while other brands will have disappeared, although they may have only been on sale for a few years.

Initially it is probably best to choose a theme. This may simply be to study the different ways that, say, strawberries have been designed on labels, or to discover how many brands of tomatoes there are and from which countries they come. Over a number of years labels will change many times, not only to conform with new laws and social changes but also to keep their design up-to-date. Conversely, it would be interesting to find those designs that deliberately retain their old-fashioned graphics.

Whatever theme is chosen, it is important to annotate each label with at least the date when it was purchased from the store and also its price. Any further information will add to the interest of the label and the collection as a whole. Imagine the delight that a social historian of the future would have on finding that the label he held was from a can of the first spaghetti to be shaped like the letters of the alphabet, or that a certain drink was thought by the press to be unfit for human consumption.

A recently discovered collection of wine labels, saved by someone in the 1950s (evidently a wine connoisseur), gave relevant details for each bottle on the back of the label. Thus for a Spanish burgundy the inscription read "13 July 1954. A remarkably good money's worth at 6/6d"; for Château Valrose "Rena (S. Kensington) 30 April 1955 9/-, recommended by the shop. Not bad really"; for La Tourelle "Holsworth — 14 August

1954 6/6d A shocking brew"; and for a Macon Superior "Remarkably good value at 6/6, wants to be well warmed. One of 6 trial bottles from Jacksons, which came by goods train, taking a month from London to Coventry. December 1954."

How to Remove Labels

The best way of removing labels from bottles or boxes is to soak them in warm water and wait for them to float off. Some assistance in peeling off the label may be necessary. When the glue is particularly strong, boiling water may be required. Once the label is detached, any excess glue should be removed and the label rinsed in cold water. It should then be gently pressed between sheets of blotting paper and, finally, put between two flat cards with a weight on top. Some glazed labels lose their shine when soaked, but this can be restored by covering the label with a clean cloth and pressing it with a warm iron.

To remove tin can labels, it is best to score through the line where the label ends overlap, using the point of a knife that is not too sharp. In most cases it is then possible to pry the label off the can. The hardened glue should be removed whenever practicable. Inevitably, some trial and error is involved.

Many collectors mount their labels in loose-leaf albums, which enable extra sheets to be added. Alternatively, they can be kept in envelopes and stored in a card index system. Three-dimensional objects should be stored in a system of boxes, preferably of the same size for ease of stacking. Any collection should be kept in a dry place, but away from heat sources such as radiators or direct sunlight.

Left Contrasting styles of label design from the 1890s. Tourist brand nicely illustrates the can opening and shows the advantages of cans for a picnic — particularly if there has been no "catch."

BIBLIOGRAPHY

Other books that include labels

Beaver, Patrick *The Match Makers*, Henry Melland Ltd, London, 1985

Buccellati, Graziella (Ed.) *Biscuits*, Franco Maria Ricci, Milan, 1982

Clark, Hyla *The Tin Can Book*, New American Library, New York, 1977

Davis, Alec *Package & Print*, Faber and Faber Ltd, London, 1967

Humbert, Claude *Label Design*, Office du Livre, Fribourg, 1972

Kovel, Ralph and Terry *Kovels Book of Antique Labels*, Crown Publishers Inc, New York

Lewis, John *Printed Ephemera*, W. S. Cowell Ltd, Ipswich, 1962

Opie, Robert *Rule Britannia*, Viking, London, 1985

Osborne, Keith and Pipe, Brian *The International Book of Beer Labels, Mats and Coasters*, Hamlyn, London, 1979

Salkin, John and Gordon, Laurie *Orange Crate Art*, Warner, New York, 1976

INDEX

Page numbers in *italic* refer to illustrations